FOUR HORSEMEN
A TIMELINE HISTORY

IN MEMORIAM

This book is dedicated to the memory of Robert Riddick, Jr. He loved the Four Horsemen, and I think he would have loved this project.

He was a great photographer, and several of his photographs appear within these pages. We had become very good friends in the years before his death and I thought of him often as I worked on this book.

FOUR HORSEMEN
A Timeline History

by Dick Bourne
Research Assistance by Brian Rogers

Copyright © 2017 by Richmond W. Bourne. All Rights Reserved. No part of this book may be reproduced or transmitted in any form or by any means, electronic or mechanical, including photocopying, recording, or by any information storage or retrieval system with out permission in writing from the author. Any unauthorized use of the material within, including text, graphics, design concepts, and photographs, without specific written consent from the author will constitute infringement of copyright.

Independently published by the Mid-Atlantic Gateway. Project concept, book layout, and cover design by Dick Bourne. For more information on this book and other books from the Mid-Atlantic Gateway, please visit us at: www.midatlanticgateway.com.

ACCAVER-4H.CS.4.2.0.BW.170514-4H.CVR.4.0.170504.BW.152

Special thanks to Brian Rogers and Kyra Quinn for their friendship and their personal commitment to this project.

For more information on other Mid-Atlantic Gateway books, visit MidAtlanticGateway.com

PHOTO CONTRIBUTIONS
(in alphabetical order)
Dick Bourne, Eddie Cheslock, Wayne Culler, Wade Keller, Robert Riddick, Jr.

Selected photos licensed through
Pro Wrestling Illustrated/Kappa Publishing.

Photographers are credited beside their photographs except the following:
Front and back cover photos of the Four Horsemen licensed from Pro Wrestling Illustrated/Kappa Publishing. Back cover photo of Barry Windham by Eddie Cheslock.

MEMORABILIA CONTRIBUTIONS
Pieces of memorabilia photographed or reproduced within these pages are from the private collections of Dick Bourne, Brian Rogers, and George South.

RESEARCH
The following were invaluable resources while doing research for this book:

Brian (Rainman) Rogers
Wrestling Results compiled by David Baker for the Mid-Atantic Gateway
Online World of Wrestling (onlineworldofwrestling.com)
The Horsemen Files (angelfire.com/ma/fourhorsemen)
Hisaharu Tanabe's Title Histories at Wrestling-Titles.com
History of the WWE (thehistoryofwwe.com)
Historians and long time fans Mark Eastridge and Carroll Hall
The WWE Network
Conversations with Jim Morrison, Marty Lunde, and Bob Caudle

EDITING
Kyra Quinn,
Peggy Lathan, and Brian Rogers

SPECIAL THANKS ALSO TO
Conrad Thompson at MLWRadio.com
Bruce Mitchell at PWTorch.com
Wade Keller at PWTorch.com
Mike Johnson at PWInsider.com
Dave Meltzer at WrestlingObserver.com
Mike Mooneyham at MikeMooneyham.com / Charleston Post & Courier
Dave Millican at DaveMillicanBelts.com
David Chappell at the Mid-Atlantic Gateway
Brack Beasley and Justin "JZ" Zimmerman

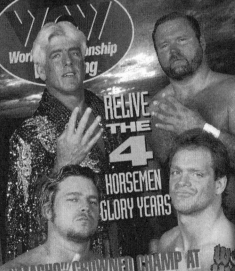

Table of Contents

Preface	A Matter of Family	10
Chapter One	The Formation of the Four Horsemen	14
Chapter Two	The Four Horsemen Through Time	20
Chapter Three	The Crockett Era	34
Chapter Four	Lightening in a Bottle	86
Chapter Five	The Early WCW Era	92
Chapter Six	The Monday Nitro Era	108
Chapter Seven	Reflections	132
Chapter Eight	Legacy	144

PREFACE
A Matter of Family

In February of 1987, Ole Anderson and James J. Dillon created a little revisionist-history when they presented a series of interviews detailing how the Horsemen originally came together. The basis of this history was that the original Four Horsemen were the Anderson family, which first consisted in the late 1960s of the greatest tag team in the history of pro-wrestling, the brother team of Gene and Ole Anderson. They were joined by their brash young cousin Ric Flair in the mid-1970s, and then later by Arn Anderson in the mid-1980s. According to Ole and J.J. in those TV interviews, these were the original Four Horsemen.

These interviews were actually part of the foundation of an angle that led to Ole Anderson being kicked out of the Four Horsemen, to be replaced by Lex Luger, a story that will be reviewed in the timeline portion of this book. I always liked the familial aspect of the Horsemen in the 1980s, the way they put their hands in together in an "all for one and one for all" act of solidarity and camaraderie. They talked about it often in those interviews over those years. They were like a family in many ways. Arn Anderson has spoken about how they might as well have been; they were with each other on the road more than they were with their own real families.

I've always treasured those 1987 interviews in a selfish way, even if they created a bit of fantasy history that never really existed. My favorite tag team of all time was the Minnesota Wrecking Crew, Gene and Ole Anderson. To hear Ole and J.J.

> *"You know, a lot of people have asked about the Four Horsemen. Let me just remind you. The Four Horsemen started with Gene and I - - talking about family. Two of the best wrestlers in the world.*
>
> *Along came another pretty good guy who later became World's Heavyweight champion. Again, family. I'm talking about Ric Flair.*
>
> *A little bit after that, a little more family moved in, and that's when we ended up with Four Horsemen when Arn stepped in. And we wrestled all over the world, the best four wrestlers in the world, the Four Horsemen. Until Gene was hurt.*
>
> *And it was at the point for the first time in the history of the Four Horsemen; we took in a man from the outside. We found a man who had all the qualifications and characteristics that were needed to be a Horseman. An outsider, but like one of the family. And I'm talking about the World's Television champion, Tully Blanchard."*
>
> *– Ole Anderson, February 1987*

in 1987 incorporate Gene Anderson, who by this time had been retired from active competition for several years, into the fabled history of the Horsemen was just one of the coolest moments ever for me as a fan.

This Four Horsemen fairy-tale was never mentioned again, and of course Gene Anderson was never a member of the Four

Horsemen. The original group in 1985 was Ric, Ole, and Arn, who hooked up with Tully and J.J. and they organically grew together as a group. However, Gene being thrown into the story had an air of plausibility and credibility to it because indeed the Horsemen had always been, and always would be, anchored by the Anderson family. Throughout all of the incarnations of the Horsemen that followed, it was the Anderson family that remained the one common denominator – the cousins Ric Flair and Arn Anderson. They were a part of every version and reformation of the Four Horsemen over the thirteen years that the Four Horsemen existed.

In this book, I will lay out a detailed timeline that documents all of those different versions of the Horsemen, the various members, their championships, the reformations, as well as those peripheral members that supported the group as valets at different points in time.

"Four Horsemen" is meant to be more of a reference book than anything else, similar to "Minnesota Wrecking Crew," my timeline book on the history of the Anderson family in wrestling. It is a place to keep up with all the personnel changes and championship developments when the Horsemen were a major part of Jim Crockett Promotions and World Championship Wrestling.

It is a story that starts off as a thrill ride but fades out sadly at the end, before finally resurrecting one final time in the Hall of Fame. ◆

> *"I'm a kiss stealin', wheelin' dealin', limosine ridin', jet flyin' son of a gun.*
> *I wear around my waist the most coveted trophy in all of professional sports - the Ten Pounds of Gold, the World Heavyweight championship.*
> *There's only one."*
> *- Ric Flair*

> He was the NWA World Heavyweight champion when the Horsemen first became a unit in 1985. A dozen or so title reigns later (depending on how you count them) he lost the WCW World title just before the Horsemen fell apart for the final time in 1999. Ric Flair was the one constant throughout all the years of the Four Horsemen.

Photograph by Wayne Culler

CHAPTER ONE
The Formation of the Four Horsemen

History will likely reflect that the greatest stable of wrestlers ever assembled were the Four Horsemen. They were the first group of their kind seen on a national stage. All the factions that followed, from the Dangerous Alliance to the nWo to Evolution, were somewhat molded in their image. They are the standard -- especially the early iterations of the group -- by which all other factions are judged.

But unlike other factions that followed, the Four Horsemen formed organically. They were not someone's creative idea. No booker sat around thinking of what four wrestlers he could throw together and what clever name he might give them.

The four men who came together to form the original group -- Ole and Arn Anderson, Ric Flair, and Tully Blanchard -- were simply four wrestlers who had common goals, common lifestyles, and common enemies.

Perhaps the earliest indication that these wrestlers were starting to come together as a group was when Tully Blanchard aided Ole and Arn Anderson in breaking Sam Houston's arm in August of 1985. Broadcaster David Crockett would refer to them as "the unholy alliance."

But even at this point in time, the four were not anywhere near a cohesive unit. Tully Blanchard's early relationship with the Anderson family and Flair mainly played out in the Georgia territory as seen on WTBS. Back in the traditional Mid-Atlantic Wrestling territory, Flair was still a "good guy" and Tully Blanchard was still his adversary. Their history went all the way back to early 1984, when Flair faced challenges from Blanchard and his partner at that time, Wahoo McDaniel. In fact, Flair was still having occasional one-on-one matches with Blanchard as late as September of 1985.

DUSTY RHODES

Sam Houston, however, was obviously not the real target. The Andersons and Blanchard used Houston to get at Dusty Rhodes, as Houston was Rhodes' young protégé. When you get right down to it, long before they called themselves the Four Horsemen, these four were bound together by their desire to eliminate the "American Dream" Dusty Rhodes.

Rhodes was their single greatest adversary. He was the kingpin. And the Andersons, Blanchard, and Flair were always looking for the opportunity to take him down. In the final analysis of their great story, one might consider Dusty Rhodes as the reason the original Four Horsemen came together to begin with.

Rhodes had separate histories with Ole Anderson and Ric Flair going back to the mid-1970s in the Mid-Atlantic and Georgia territories. And in this year of 1985, Dusty had taken his other young protégé, Magnum T.A. and formed "America's Team" and the two of them had various singles and tag team battles with Flair, Ole, Arn, and Tully throughout that whole year.

THE CAGE IN ATLANTA

The key event that started the wheels in motion was that infamous night in late September when Flair turned his back on Rhodes in the steel cage in Atlanta.

The first pieces of that developed when Dusty offered aid to Flair in his battle with the Russians. Flair warned Dusty at that point to stay out of his business, but Rhodes failed to heed that warning and on September 29, 1985, in the Omni in Atlanta, he paid the price for it.

Flair had just defeated Nikita Koloff inside a steel cage to successfully defend the NWA World championship. Ivan Koloff had entered the cage and both of the Russians were ganging up on Flair. Suddenly Rhodes entered the cage to a huge ovation to help Flair once again and he cleared the ring of the Russians. Flair seemed furious. Moments later the Andersons entered the cage and attacked Rhodes. If fans thought for a moment that Flair might return the favor and lend a hand to Dusty, they soon learned otherwise. The Andersons locked the cage door and held Rhodes down on the mat as Flair came off the top rope down on his leg, breaking his ankle. The good-guy locker room emptied as Magnum T.A., Ricky Morton, Robert Gibson, and Terry Taylor all tried to scale the cage walls. But the Andersons kept knocking them down. The Omni crowd began to riot. With that crazy scene in the Omni, the seeds were sewn for what would become the battle of the Horsemen vs. Dusty Rhodes over the next several years.

Soon after the cage massacre in Atlanta, Tully Blanchard became tightly aligned with Flair and the Andersons. He had spent the first half of 1985 battling Rhodes over the TV title and the second half battling Magnum T.A. over the United States title. Earlier that July, he had watched as the Andersons jumped Magnum alone in a locker room and left him broken and unable to compete. And now he watched Flair and the Andersons have their way with Dusty in the steel cage. Tully calculated that it made sense to align himself politically with "the family."

The four of them now, with Baby Doll still at Tully's side, began to be seen with each other on television interviews, and Tully began teaming regularly with the Andersons in six man tag matches around the country.

It was in early October that Arn Anderson began talking about the four of them as a unit, referring to them as the "elite group" in professional wrestling. It is believed that at some point around this same time Arn first coined the phrase "four horsemen" to describe the group.

> *"Not since the four horsemen of the apocalypse have so few wreaked so much havoc on so many."*
> *- Arn Anderson*

While it has been suggested that this biblical reference took place during an interview on one of Jim Crockett's nationally televised programs, I have always believed that it happened in a local promo, one of the hundreds that were taped each week during those years at the makeshift studio on Briarbend Drive in Charlotte. If it had happened during the body of one of the main TV programs, footage of that interview would have surfaced by now. The WWE owns the entire Crockett Promotions video library and the reference by Arn has never shown up in any of the Horsemen documentaries, DVDs, or the WWE Network.

Arn Anderson confirmed that theory in a conversation I had with him in the late summer of 2015 in Huntsville, AL.

"Yes, it was on a local promo," Arn told me. "And in fact, I just said it off the cuff, not really intending to be coming up with a name for us or anything like that."

Arn went further with another tidbit of information that we had not heard before that moment. "It was Tony Schiavone who actually validated the whole thing," he said. "He looked at me after the promo was over and said, 'I think you just named yourself.' And that led to us starting to refer to ourselves as the Four Horsemen."

"The Enforcer" Arn Anderson
Arn was one half of the National Tag Team champions with Ole Anderson
in 1985 when he gave the Four Horsemen their name.
(Photograph by Eddie Cheslock)

Arn first classified them as the Four Horsemen on national television (as opposed to those local promos) on the November 9, 1985, Saturday night episode of "World Championship Wrestling." As United States heavyweight champion Tully Blanchard waited in the ring with Baby Doll for his scheduled TV match, Arn was doing an interview at the podium with Tony Schiavone and said the following:

> *"What you've got right here in the ring, you've got a champion; you've got Tully Blanchard. You've got Ole Anderson. You've got myself, and last but by no means least, you've got Ric Flair, the World's Heavyweight champion. You're talking about the 'four horsemen' of professional wrestling - - the people that make things happen." - Arn Anderson*

Tully became a regular partner of the Andersons in six-man tag matches in October and November and, after Starrcade, teamed several times during the month of December with Ric Flair against Dusty and Magnum.

The four were now all closely associated with each other, but just as fans had started to pick up on the name of the Four Horsemen, Dusty Rhodes got revenge for the cage attack that past September. He and the Road Warriors broke Ole Anderson's leg in a six-man tag team match on New Year's night at the Omni in Atlanta. Ole was out of action for 5 months. During that time, David Crockett would occasionally mock the group referring to them as the "three horsemen."

When Ole returned in early June of 1986, the Four Horsemen were in full force again. And with James J. Dillon as their manager (and a personnel change or two along the way) they would dominate Jim Crockett Promotions for the next three years. ◆

CHAPTER TWO
The Four Horsemen Through Time

Within this book, the history of the Four Horsemen is divided into three distinct sections called 'eras."

ERAS OF THE HORSEMEN		
Crockett Era	1985-1989	The Originals
Early WCW Era	1989-1993	Reformations 1 & 2
Monday Nitro Era	1995-1999	Reformations 3 & 4

The first of these is called "The Crockett Era." It was within that time period when the Four Horsemen flourished as a unit.

It's not too controversial a position to take that this first era is the most important and significant time period in their history. Everything that followed those early versions of the Horsemen didn't seem to look or feel quite the same to one degree or another. However, each subsequent version of the Horsemen is an important part of the whole story. It just might not be as exciting as those first versions in that first era.

The second is 'The Early WCW Era." This time period begins with the first reformation of the Horsemen in late 1989, which fell during the first year of Ted Turner's stewardship over the company he purchased in late 1988. It continues through the turbulent early years of the new company that would become known as WCW.

The third and final era is "The Monday Nitro Era." Named for the flagship program of the company that first aired in 1995 on Turner's TNT Network, this time period coincides with the 'Monday night wars' between WCW and the WWF. While the company rose to new heights during the early years of this era, the Horsemen endured their most dysfunctional time period ever, leading to their ultimate demise.

The Timeline

When I began kicking around ideas for a book project on the Four Horsemen, I first thought I would compile a detailed account of the Crockett era alone. It was the period that most interested me, and it is certainly the period most fondly remembered by fans.

However, friends suggested to me that with so much confusion out there about the events that followed that first era of the Horsemen, it would be helpful to include an account of each version that followed the originals, to clarify when things happened and exactly who was and wasn't a member of the group. When I began thinking of it in that way, I decided to put together a timeline similar to the approach in my book "Minnesota Wrecking Crew," which is a timeline history of the Anderson family in pro wrestling.

The decision to do the timeline meant that this book would be more of a reference work, a book of facts on a linear timeline,

THE FOUR HORSEMEN OF THE APOCALYPSE

When Arn Anderson first used the phrase "four horsemen" to reference the coming together of the Four Horsemen of wrestling, he was actually making a reference to the Four Horsemen of the Apocalypse from the New Testament book of Revelation in the Bible.

In the 6th chapter of Revelation, seven seals are broken on a scroll in the right hand of God, the first four of which summon beings who ride on different color horses. They are symbolic descriptions of different events that will take place at the end of time. The four riders represent conquest, war, famine, and death.

Arn compares what he and the boys were planning for Dusty Rhodes and crew to the wrath the biblical horsemen would unleash on the world. While there is no direct quote of what Arn said, it is generally thought to have been something like this:

> *"Not since the four horsemen of the apocalypse have so few wreaked so much havoc on so many." - Arn Anderson*

It was amazing, powerful imagery that stuck with the group, and of course eventually became their name.

THE FOUR HORSEMEN OF NOTRE DAME

In popular culture in the early 1900s, the term "four horsemen" became attached to the famous college football backfield of the University of Notre Dame. It happened when legendary sportswriter Grantland Rice wrote about a 1924 gridiron battle between the Fighting Irish and the Cadets of Army in the New York Herald Tribune. It is one of the most famous passages in sports:

> Outlined against a blue-gray October sky, the Four Horsemen rode again. In dramatic lore their names are Death, Destruction, Pestilence, and Famine. But those are aliases. Their real names are: Stuhldreher, Crowley, Miller and Layden. They formed the crest of the South Bend cyclone before which another fighting Army team was swept over the precipice at the Polo Grounds this afternoon as 55,000 spectators peered down upon the bewildering panorama spread out upon the green plain below.

I still get chills reading that today.

The name caught on with the help of a publicity photograph placing the players on four horses. A statue was commissioned based on the photograph, which stands today on the campus of Notre Dame University in South Bend, IN.

The Four Horsemen of Notre Dame are still a cherished part of Notre Dame football lore nearly a century later. ◆

rather than the written story of the Four Horsemen. I enjoy history presented in that fashion. There are actually some very good written histories out there online, and there is the WWE's video documentary on the Horsemen that is fairly comprehensive as well. But within each of those, there are discrepancies and certain things that don't make sense or simply aren't true. Sometimes history is rewritten out of convenience or agenda. Sometimes our memories are just fuzzy. The finer points and small details of wrestling history are hard for anyone to nail down, but that is part of what makes it fun. And that is what I try to do here.

I have attempted to be as thorough and accurate as possible, but I'm sure there may be a few mistakes here or there and some points that could be debated. I welcome all corrections and arguments, as I know that a lot folks take their Horsemen history very seriously. So do I.

THE HORSEMEN ROSTER
MEMBERSHIP LIST

NAME	ERA	YEARS	ROLE
Ric Flair	Crockett, Early WCW, Monday Nitro	1985-1999	Wrestler
Ole Anderson	Crockett, Early WCW	1985-1987, 1989-1990, 1993*	Wrestler, Manager
Arn Anderson	Crockett, Early WCW, Monday Nitro	1985-1999	Wrestler, Manager
Tully Blanchard	Crockett	1985-1988	Wrestler
Baby Doll	Crockett	1985, 1986	Valet
James J. Dillon	Crockett	1985-1989, 1998*	Manager, Occasional Wrestler
Lex Luger	Crockett	1987	Wrestler
Dark Journey	Crockett	1987	Valet
Barry Windham	Crockett, Early WCW	1988-1989, 1990-1991	Wrestler
Kendall Windham	Crockett	1989	Wrestler
Sting	Early WCW	1989-1990	Wrestler
Woman	Early WCW, Monday Nitro	1990, 1996-1997	Valet
Sid Vicious	Early WCW	1990-1991	Wrestler
Paul Roma	Early WCW	1993	Wrestler
Brian Pillman	Monday Nitro	1995-1996	Wrestler
Chris Benoit	Monday Nitro	1995-1999	Wrestler
Miss Elizabeth	Monday Nitro	1996	Valet
Steve McMichael	Monday Nitro	1996-1999	Wrestler
Debra McMichael	Monday Nitro	1996-1997	Valet
Jeff Jarrett	Monday Nitro	1997	Wrestler
Curt Hennig	Monday Nitro	1997	Wrestler
Dean Malenko	Monday Nitro	1998-1999	Wrestler

* One night only.

Membership and Championships

Primary emphasis within the timeline is on the events that lead to personnel changes within the Four Horsemen, locking down exact dates of when wrestlers entered and exited the group. The stories behind those changes are also covered, to the extent that there is a story to tell.

Championship wins and losses are included. These title changes are only listed for wrestlers when they were active members of the Four Horsemen. Title changes for wrestlers when they were not members of the Horsemen are not included.

The Roster

The chart on the facing page lists all of the members of the Four Horsemen over the years. The primary members, of course, are the wrestlers. But also included here are the managers as well as the women who were officially affiliated with the Horsemen over the years.

There were several people who lent a hand to the Horsemen over the years. They will be included in their own chart later in the book, and are mentioned in the timeline.

A Summary of Horsemen History

On the next five pages you will find charts summarizing the many personnel moves that defined the various versions of the Four Horsemen over time. It is divided into the three main eras defined earlier. The detailed timeline that documents each of these changes in the Horsemen unfolds in the chapters that follow.

It is my hope that wrestling fans of all ages and from all generations will find something of interest within these chapters, and that the timeline will help put the thirteen year saga of the Four Horsemen in sharper perspective. ◆

THE CROCKETT ERA
(1985-1988)

THE ORIGINAL FOUR HORSEMEN
(aka THE OLE ANDERSON VERSION)

October 1985 – December 1985
The original Four Horsemen come together.
Ric Flair, Ole Anderson, Arn Anderson, Tully Blanchard
Baby Doll (Valet)

January 1986 – May 1986
Ole Anderson injured. James J. Dillon joins Tully Blanchard Enterprises. Baby Doll goes with Dusty Rhodes
Ric Flair, Ole Anderson, Arn Anderson, Tully Blanchard
James J. Dillon (Admin. Director of Tully Blanchard Enterprises)

June 1986 – February 1987
First time all four are in action with J.J. Dillon as manager.
Ric Flair, Ole Anderson, Arn Anderson, Tully Blanchard
James J. Dillon (executive director of the Four Horsemen)

THE LEX LUGER VERSION

January 1987 – February 1987
Horsemen take on Lex Luger as an associate member.
Ric Flair, Ole Anderson, Arn Anderson, Tully Blanchard
Lex Luger (associate of the Four Horsemen)
James J. Dillon (executive director of the Four Horsemen)

March 1987 – December 1987
Lex Luger made official member. Ole Anderson is kicked out.
Ric Flair, Arn Anderson, Tully Blanchard, Lex Luger
James J. Dillon (executive director of the Four Horsemen)

Dark Journey joins the group in May 1987 as Tully Blanchard's "executive secretary." She is gone by early-August.

Ric Flair, Arn Anderson, Tully Blanchard, Lex Luger
James J. Dillon (Executive Director of the Four Horsemen)
Dark Journey (Executive Secretary)

**December 1987 – April 1988
Lex Luger leaves the Four Horsemen.**

Ric Flair, Arn Anderson, Tully Blanchard
James J. Dillon (Executive Director of the Four Horsemen)

THE BARRY WINDHAM VERSION

**April 1988 – September 1988
Barry Windham joins the group after turning on Lex Luger.**

Ric Flair, Arn Anderson, Tully Blanchard, Barry Windham
James J. Dillon (Executive Director)

**September 1988 – January 1989
Tully Blanchard & Arn Anderson leave for the WWF.**

Ric Flair, Barry Windham
James J. Dillon (Executive Director)

**Late January 1989 – Early February 1989
Kendall Windham joins his brother in the Four Horsemen.**

Ric Flair, Barry Windham, Kendall Windham
James J. Dillon (Executive Director)

**The Four Horsemen go dormant.
February 1989 – December 1989**

Hiro Matsuda of the Yamazaki Corporation of Japan purchases the contracts of the Horsemen.

EARLY WCW ERA
(1989-1993)

REFORMATION #1
Sting • Barry Windham • Sid Vicious

December 1989 – February 1990
Arn Anderson returns to WCW to re-form the Horsemen with Ric Flair and Ole Anderson. Sting is made a member at Starrcade '89.

Ric Flair, Ole Anderson, Arn Anderson, Sting

February 1990 – April 1990
Sting kicked out. Woman becomes a valet.

Ric Flair, Ole Anderson, Arn Anderson
Woman (Valet)

April 1990
Barry Windham returns to WCW and reunites with the Horsemen.

Ric Flair, Ole Anderson, Arn Anderson, Barry Windham
Woman (Valet)

May 1990 – May 1991
Sid Vicious joins. Ole Anderson becomes their manager.

Ric Flair, Arn Anderson, Barry Windham, Sid Vicious
Ole Anderson (manager until July 1990)
Woman (Valet) (leaves the group after Sid Vicious joins)

The Four Horsemen go dormant.
June 1991 – May 1993

Ric Flair and Sid Vicious leave for the WWF.

REFORMATION #2
Paul Roma

May 1993 – November 1993
Paul Roma joins the group at Slamboree '93

Ric Flair, Arn Anderson, Paul Roma
Ole Anderson (*one night only)

The Four Horsemen go dormant.
December 1993 - October 1995

Paul Roma turns on Arn Anderson.

THE MONDAY NITRO ERA
(1995-1999)

REFORMATION #3
Pillman • Benoit • McMichael • Jarrett • Hennig

October 1995
Horsemen re-formed after Flair swerves Sting. Brian Pillman joins the group.

Ric Flair, Arn Anderson, Brian Pillman

November 1995
Chris Benoit joins as the fourth Horsemen.

Ric Flair, Arn Anderson, Brian Pillman, Chris Benoit

February 1996
Pillman fired from WCW. Woman and Miss Elizabeth become Horsemen valets.

Ric Flair, Arn Anderson, Chris Benoit
with Woman and Miss Elizabeth (Valets)

June 1996
Steve "Mongo" McMichael joins. Debra becomes a valet.

Ric Flair, Arn Anderson, Chris Benoit, Steve McMichael
with Woman, Miss Elizabeth, Queen Debra (Valets)

February 1997
Jeff Jarrett defeats Mongo to earn a spot in the Horseman.

Ric Flair, Arn Anderson, Chris Benoit, Steve McMichael, Jeff Jarrett
with Woman and Debra McMichael (Valets)

June 1997
Jeff Jarrett is kicked out of the Four Horsemen

Ric Flair, Arn Anderson, Chris Benoit, Steve McMichael

August 1997
Arn Anderson gives Curt Hennig his spot in the Four Horsemen

Ric Flair, Chris Benoit, Steve McMichael, Curt Hennig
Arn Anderson (no longer active, serves in a managerial role)

Ten Pounds of Gold
This was the NWA World title belt that Ric Flair wore and defended during the early days of the Four Horsemen. The belt was retired in February of 1986.

September 1997
Curt Hennig turns on the Horsemen and joins the nWo

Ric Flair, Chris Benoit, Steve McMichael
Arn Anderson (no longer active, serves in a managerial role)

The Four Horsemen go dormant.
October 1997

With lots of injuries followed by backstage politics, the Horsemen take separate paths and are inactive as a group until the final reformation in 1998.

REFORMATION #4
The Final Version of the Four Horsemen

September 1998 - May 1999
James J. Dillon and Arn Anderson reunite the Four Horsemen.
Dean Malenko made a member.

Ric Flair, Chris Benoit, Steve McMichael, Dean Malenko
Arn Anderson (manager)
James J. Dillon* (one night only: Greenville Nitro)

The Four Horsemen go dormant. Forever.
May 1999

Mongo leaves WCW. Benoit and Malenko part ways with Ric Flair. Arn remains loyal to Flair until the bitter end.

Facing page: Arn and Ole Anderson were National Tag Team champions at the time of the formation of the Four Horsemen in 1985.
(Photograph by Eddie Cheslock)

NOTES TO THE READER

Assumptions made when writing the timeline: The timeline is written with certain assumptions that the reader is generally familiar with the history, characters, and storylines within Jim Crockett Promotions and World Championship Wrestling during the time period covered.

A note about Arn's storyline relationship to Ole: Over the course of many years, beginning in 1982 and going all the way into the early 1990s, Arn was at different times represented as the nephew, brother, or cousin of Ole Anderson. The nephew relationship was the earliest connection, devised by Georgia booker Ole Anderson in 1982 to make Marty Lunde an Anderson to begin with. That was in the Georgia territory, and Arn would keep the name and the nephew relationship while he worked elsewhere, primarily in the Southeast territory in 1983 and 1984. It wasn't until 1985 when Arn first came to work for Jim Crockett Promotions that storyline confusion set in. Apparently booker Dusty Rhodes liked the brother relationship from a storyline standpoint because he had his own twelve year history of feuding with Gene and Ole, "the Anderson Brothers." It just felt right to call Ole and Arn the "Anderson Brothers." But that didn't make much sense given the age difference between the two, and Ole, Arn, and Ric would all be called cousins at different times. The brother relationship hung around, though, as by 1990 when they were feuding with the Steiner brothers, Ole and Arn were billed as a brother team once again. It never seemed to matter one way or the other to fans, though.

Where references are directly made to family relationships within the extended Anderson family, it is understood that the references are part of the wrestling story being told, then and now.

A note about storyline: The timeline is generally a reference to booking and storyline events. Where references are made to real or behind-the-scenes events, they will be acknowledged as such. However, it is exceedingly difficult to tell the story of pro-wrestling without occasionally swerving in and out between reality and storyline and between 'work' and 'shoot.'

A note about references to Jim Crockett Promotions and WCW as the "NWA": Although the NWA (National Wrestling Alliance) was still legally and technically a separate organization during the period of time covered in this book, it is understood that "NWA" will be used in the same way Jim Crockett Promotions and later the Ted Turner wrestling organization would refer to itself before abandoning the NWA moniker and re-branded everything "WCW". "NWA" in this book will refer to the Crockett and Turner promotions and not the organization of affiliated promoters.

A note about references to the WWE: References to the WWE (World Wrestling Entertainment) are made within the context of the company's name ('WWF' or 'WWE') at the time of the reference.

A note about references to injuries: When referring to a wrestler's injuries within the timeline, every effort will be made to differentiate between a "worked" injury for storyline purposes, or an actual legitimate ("shoot") injury. If no reference is made, it can be assumed that injury is part of a storyline.

A note about the Yamazaki Corporation: Throughout many published references, both in print and online, Hiro Matsuda's storyline faction is spelled both "Yamazaki Corporation" and "Yamasaki Corporation." Within this book, it will be spelled in the former.

A note about Baby Doll: Throughout many published references, both in print and online, Baby Doll is spelled both as one word ("Babydoll") and two words ("Baby Doll") I have used 'Babydoll' in the past but have come to believe that the correct usage is the two word spelling. "Baby Doll" will be used in this book.

A note about 'versions' and 'reformations': For purposes the discussion within the book, a 'reformation' of the Four Horsemen takes place only after a period of dormancy. A 'version' refers to the various different line-ups within any reformation or era, and can be distinguished by a replacement, addition, or subtraction of an individual to the group outside of a transition period.

A note about repetitive naming and information: Some bits of information between entries in the timeline are repeated. The timeline is written to be a reference guide where most individual entries to the timeline would stand on their own without necessarily having the context of other entries.

The term 'manager' may represent at different times a manager, executive director, advisor, leader, etc.

The term 'valet' is the general classification chosen to represent the women who were directly affiliated with the Horsemen over time as a group, even if that term was never used for them individually at the time being covered, and without regard to the fact they were much more than valets.

A note about Chris Benoit: It has sometimes been difficult to write about Chris and Nancy Benoit within the context of these storylines as if the horrific events of 2007 had not even happened. I am mindful that they did, and how painful it is for many people to be reminded of it. The Horsemen history, however, preceded all of that and it is written as it happened at the time. Now almost 10 years later as I write this, our condolences continue to be extended to their families and friends. ◆

TIMELINE

CHAPTER THREE
The Crockett Era
1985-1989

As the timeline begins, we start with the main angle most closely associated with the formation of the Four Horsemen, the attack of Dusty Rhodes inside the steel cage in the Omni in Atlanta.

It seemed that the entire year of 1985 had been building to this very moment. Even though loosely allied in the Mid-Atlantic area, tensions still ran high between Ric Flair and Dusty Rhodes following their world title clash at Starrcade '84 a year earlier. Rhodes had battled Tully Blanchard for much of the spring and early summer over the TV title, and along with Magnum T.A. had fought the Andersons into the early fall.

Everything was getting ready to come to a head. All of Dusty's enemies would soon be aligned against him, and from that alignment, the Four Horsemen would be born.

1985

SEPTEMBER 1985
Ric Flair defeats Nikita Koloff in a cage at the Omni in Atlanta, GA, to retain the NWA World Championship. After the match, Ivan Koloff and Krusher Khrushchev enter the ring and pummel Flair until Dusty Rhodes makes the save. Flair turns on Dusty and is joined by Ole and Arn Anderson and they break Dusty's leg.

A loose relationship develops between "the family" (the Andersons and Flair) and Tully Blanchard, which leads to Blanchard occasionally teaming with the Andersons in six-man matches.

OCTOBER 1985
On the 10/12 edition of "World Championship Wrestling," Arn Anderson makes his first reference to what he would eventually dub the Four Horsemen:

> "As you know, Tony Schiavone and David Crockett, I run with the world heavyweight champion Ric Flair, Tully Blanchard, and Ole Anderson. That's an elite group in all the world." – Arn Anderson

On the 10/19 edition of "World Championship Wrestling," Arn kicks the crutches out from under Dusty Rhodes and, with the help of Tully Blanchard, steals the World TV title belt from him as well.

NOVEMBER 1985
On WTBS's Saturday night "World Championship Wrestling" airing 11/9, Arn Anderson makes his first WTBS reference to the Four Horsemen in an interview with Tony Schiavone, as Tully Blanchard (with Baby Doll) is in the ring waiting for his match to begin:

> "What you've got right here in the ring, you've got a champion; you've got Tully Blanchard. You've got Ole Anderson. You've got myself, and last but by no means least, you've got Ric Flair, the World's Heavyweight champion. You're talking about the 'four horsemen' of professional wrestling - - the people that make things happen." - Arn Anderson

PERFECT 10

When you think of the original grouping of the Four Horsemen, you tend to think of the Andersons, Flair, and Blanchard with James J. Dillon. But it was actually Baby Doll who was first associated with the Horsemen during the earliest stages of their formation. Baby Doll had two very brief stints associated with the Four Horsemen about one year apart, both times with the original four.

In 1985, she became the valet of Tully Blanchard; he called her his "Perfect 10." She had been with him since January and had been a key part of that year's storylines revolving around Blanchard's feuds with Dusty Rhodes and Magnum T.A. When Tully became aligned with Flair and the Andersons that fall and the Horsemen idea began to develop, Baby Doll, by virtue of her association with Blanchard, had the benefit of being the first valet associated with the group, although she really was only closely associated with Tully.

This first short stint with the Horsemen ended in late December 1985 when James J. Dillon engineered a split between Blanchard and Baby Doll over a misunderstanding having to do with a Christmas gift. Dillon swiftly capitalized on the split between Blanchard and Baby Doll and became the "executive director" of Tully Blanchard Enterprises, and then later the leader of the Four Horsemen. Meanwhile, Baby Doll aligned herself with the American Dream.

Less than a year later, her second stint with the group began, developing during a famous televised NWA title match between Rhodes and Ric Flair in Charlotte. Baby Doll turned on the Dream and assisted Flair in the match, which ultimately led to Flair retaining the NWA title. The commentary for the match led you to believe Flair had no idea what Baby Doll was up to at first. But when fans in the

Charlotte Coliseum realized it, they nearly rioted, especially when Blanchard hit the ring and went after Rhodes's previously injured leg with a steel chair. When it was all said and done, Baby Doll left arm-in-arm with both Flair and Blanchard, although her association with the Horsemen in the weeks after her turn was more with Flair than with the others, and ended all together about a month later. ◆

Horsemen Title Change
At "Starrcade '85" on Thanksgiving night in Greensboro, NC, Magnum T.A. defeats Tully Blanchard (with Baby Doll) for the United States championship in an "I Quit" match inside a steel cage.

Also at Starrcade (but at the event in Atlanta), Dusty Rhodes defeats Ric Flair to apparently win the NWA World Heavyweight championship. The decision is reversed days later by the NWA.

On 11/30 in Richmond, VA, Ric Flair and Tully Blanchard unite to team against Dusty Rhodes and Magnum T.A. The heat that existed between Flair and Blanchard during the years 1984 and most of 1985 is now clearly behind them, as Blanchard is now completely aligned with Flair and the Andersons. Flair and Blanchard team several more times in December.

> *"When you look at Ric Flair, you have to start thinking about the family. I'm talking about Ric Flair and the Andersons. And really, you almost have to include that guy back over there, Tully Blanchard." - David Crockett*

DECEMBER 1985
In an angle taped 12/15 in Greensboro, but that did not air until 1/4/86 on "World Wide Wrestling," Tully Blanchard confronts Baby Doll as to her whereabouts over the last few weeks. The confusion surrounds an airline ticket Baby Doll thought Tully had given her for Christmas

via James J. Dillon. When Dillon denies any knowledge of the ticket, Tully suspects she's been unfaithful and slaps her across the face. Dusty Rhodes makes the save and Baby Doll aligns herself with Rhodes from that point forward. Dusty refers to Baby Doll as his "personal."

Reading between the lines, it's clear to fans that J.J. set Baby Doll up to build distrust between her and Tully. It worked beautifully, and by Tully breaking ties with Baby Doll, James J. Dillon had a new client in Tully Blanchard, replacing the departed Buddy Landel. Dillon would now be the "administrative director" for Tully Blanchard Enterprises.

1986

JANUARY 1986
On New Year's Night at the Omni in Atlanta, GA, Dusty Rhodes and the Road Warriors defeat Ric Flair and the Andersons in a six-man tag team main event. After the match, Dusty breaks Ole Anderson's leg, putting Ole out of action for 5 months and gaining revenge for what happened to him three months earlier in the very same ring.

On the 1/4 episode of "World Championship Wrestling," Tully Blanchard mentions the Four Horsemen in the context of Arn Anderson coining the phrase:

> *"Talk about the head of the family, well I tell you what: they took down one of the Four Horsemen. You know, Arn likes to say 'the Four Horsemen' - - Tully Blanchard, Ric Flair, Ole and Arn Anderson - - that's where professional wrestling revolves right there, right around those four people. You take one down, that leaves three left. But the fourth one will be back, I can guarantee you that." – Tully Blanchard*

On this same show, Tully Blanchard and James J. Dillon make their first WTBS appearance together following the split of Blanchard with Baby Doll. Tully and J.J. talk about their union:

> *"The National heavyweight championship belt that J.J. once proudly had in his trophy case, put his faith in someone a little*

James J. Dillon, the Executive Director of Tully Blanchard Enterprises, with the National Heavyweight champion Tully Blanchard
(Photograph by Robert Riddick, Jr.)

bit inferior, got beat, got took down, short lived. But I tell you what, J.J.'s on the first run team now, and it's going to really be something to see."- Tully Blanchard

"I have severed all ties with all other individuals to assume the position of administrative director for Tully Blanchard Enterprises." – James J. Dillon

Horsemen Title Change:
Arn Anderson defeats Wahoo McDaniel on 1/4/86 in Greensboro, NC, in the finals of a one-night tournament to fill the vacant NWA World TV Championship. The title had been officially vacant since October 1985 when Dusty Rhodes was stripped of the title after being unable to defend it following his ankle injury at the hands of the cage ambush in the Omni in Atlanta on 9/29/85. Arn defeated Jimmy Valiant and Ronnie Garvin on the road to the finals.

FEBRUARY 1986

Horsemen Title Change:
Ole and Arn Anderson are stripped of the National Tag Team championships after their failure to defend them in 30 days. The failure to defend was a result of Ole Anderson's injury on 1/1 in the Omni at the hands of Dusty Rhodes and the Road Warriors. Jim Crockett, Jr. makes the announcement on the 2/2 edition of "World Championship Wrestling."

Ric Flair debuts the brand new NWA World Heavyweight championship belt at Florida's "Battle of the Belts II" in Orlando. Flair first appears with the new belt on the Crockett syndicated shows on 2/22. The belt would become commonly known by fans as "the big gold belt." It was an icon closely associated with Ric Flair and the Horsemen during the Crockett era.

MARCH 1986

Horsemen Title Change:
Tully Blanchard defeats Dusty Rhodes for the National Heavyweight Championship on 3/4 in Spartanburg, SC. The match is taped as a special segment for television following the regular tapings of "Mid-Atlantic Championship Wrestling" and "World Wide Wrestling." Ric Flair is the

special color commentator with Tony Schiavone at ringside, and after the match the Horsemen gang up on Baby Doll. Tully and Arn hold her down on the mat as Ric climbs to the top rope and prepares to jump off on her, a scene reminiscent of the night they broke Dusty's leg in Atlanta. Magnum T.A. and the Rock and Roll Express make the save in one of the wildest, most heated moments you will ever see.

APRIL 1986
Ric Flair begins a feud with Ricky Morton, one half of the Rock and Roll Express tag team, drawing big crowds for their title matches over the next few months.

Flair also retains his NWA World Heavyweight Championship against Dusty Rhodes at the inaugural Jim Crockett, Sr. Memorial Cup on 4/19 at the Superdome in New Orleans, LA.

JUNE 1986
On the episode of "World Wide Wrestling" that airs 6/7, Ric Flair defends the NWA title against Dusty Rhodes in Spartanburg, SC. As Rhodes looks to be on the verge of victory, Arn and Tully hit the ring and the three do a number on Dusty before the Rock and Roll Express and Magnum T.A. make the save. Suddenly without any hint or warning, Ole Anderson makes his return, joining the fray and gaining the advantage on Rhodes and crew. The Four Horsemen celebrate their reunion, and Ole Anderson delivers one of his most memorable interviews ever:

> "I heard someone out there saying, 'Maybe our eyes are deceiving us. Maybe it's just someone that looks like Anderson. Maybe our TV is messed up. Maybe a pig can fly!' Well there ain't no maybes about it, David Crockett. You're looking at the Four Horsemen. We're back together. ... Did you really think, did you really think that you were gonna get rid of the Horsemen? Did you really think that Ole Anderson was going to go off to the sawmill and sit for the rest of his life? I'll tell you this, Rhodes. There's no way that it's gonna be over - - I know it now - - there's no way it's gonna be over until one of us is dead and buried. And right now you're looking at the burial team, you're looking at the team that's got the shovels, we've got the plot of ground out there. And you might as well realize

it, and everybody in the world better realize it - - this ain't no joke, this ain't no funnin', this is no April Fool's; I'm as serious as I can be. We're going to get rid of Dusty Rhodes. You bank on it, you go down and you can bet on it. I don't care who helps him, I don't care where, I don't know when, all I know is it's gonna be done. But right now, we're gonna do a little celebrating, because the Four Horsemen are back in business!"
– Ole Anderson

The familiar image of the Horsemen with all of their hands in together is first cemented here, and would become a customary scene within the group over next several years.

On the 6/21 edition of "World Championship Wrestling," the Four Horsemen jump the Road Warriors and leave them laying in the WTBS studio. Even though it is 4-on-2, it is still unusual to see the Road Warriors get dominated quite this badly.

JULY 1986
Horsemen Title Change:
Dusty Rhodes defeats Ric Flair for the NWA World Heavyweight championship on 7/26 at the "Great American Bash" show in Greensboro,

NC. It was the 13th match in 14 scheduled title defenses by Flair during the 1986 Great American Bash tour.

Five days later on 7/31 in Kansas City, KS at a TV taping at Memorial Hall for the Central States territory's "All Star Wrestling" program, Dusty Rhodes defends his newly won world championship against former champion Ric Flair. Flair goes hard after the previously injured leg of Dusty Rhodes, making it clear that this is his strategy to try and regain the title. Flair is disqualified and a rematch is set for the following week at the same venue. (Jim Crockett, Jr. is ringside with the NWA belt as a guest of broadcasters Kevin Wall and Rick Stewart. Jim Crockett Promotions was in the process of taking over the Central States promotion.)

AUGUST 1986

One week later on Thursday 8/7 in another rematch in the same Kansas City ring, James J. Dillon and Tully Blanchard ambush Dusty Rhodes in the ring before his title defense against Ric Flair. The incident was again part of Kansas City's "All Star Wrestling" TV taping that night and highlights are shown on WTBS on Saturday 8/9. Blanchard is there ostensibly on a clothes-buying trip to Michael's of Kansas City, one of the Horsemen's favorite places to have their custom made clothes made. He enters the ring to challenge Rhodes for a title match should Rhodes get past Flair that night. But it quickly breaks down as a Horseman ambush as Blanchard repeatedly bashes Rhodes' previously injured ankle with a steel chair, making Rhodes vulnerable in his big title defense two nights later in St. Louis.

Horsemen Title Change:
Ric Flair regains the NWA World Heavyweight Championship on 8/9 in St. Louis, MO. It was announced at the time as Flair's 4th NWA title victory. The win was set up by the ambush of Rhodes in Kansas City, KS, two days earlier.

Two weeks later in Charlotte, NC, Baby Doll turns on Dusty Rhodes and helps Ric Flair retain the NWA World title in a re-match televised on "NWA Pro Wrestling." The surprising turn came out of nowhere and created a near riot at the Charlotte Coliseum. The match took place on 8/17 and aired on television 8/23.

Photograph by Dick Bourne

World famous Michael's of Kansas City, MO, is the place the Horsemen bought their best clothes in the mid -1980s. It was mentioned many times during their interviews on Superstation WTBS.

August isn't a good month for the "American Dream," losing both his World championship and his "personal" to the "Nature Boy" Ric Flair.

Baby Doll hangs with Flair and the Horsemen for the next month or so before leaving for the Kansas City territory (now run by the Crocketts) to manage the Warlord, and after that is no longer associated with the Horsemen.

The Andersons begin feuding with the Rock and Roll Express (Ricky Morton and Robert Gibson) for a period of several months, that eventually includes a chase for the NWA World Tag Team titles.

Horsemen Title Change:
Wahoo McDaniel defeats Tully Blanchard for the National Heavyweight Championship on 8/28 at the Forum in Los Angeles, CA.

SEPTEMBER 1986
Horsemen Title Change
Dusty Rhodes defeats Arn Anderson on 9/9 in Columbia, SC, for the NWA World TV Championship. The match is the main event of "NWA Pro Wrestling" that aired on 9/13.

OCTOBER 1986
Dusty Rhodes injures the knee of Tully Blanchard during a match on 10/11 in Greensboro, NC.

The weekend of 10/18, video is shown of the Horsemen -- Ole, Arn, J.J., and Tully (on crutches) -- following Dusty in his car to the offices of Jim Crockett Promotions on Briarbend Drive. They jump him in the parking lot, tie him to a truck, and attempt to break his arm.

Only 5 days after Magnum T.A.'s career-ending automobile accident on 10/14 in Charlotte, Nikita Koloff makes his babyface turn to team with Dusty Rhodes against the Horsemen team of Ole Anderson and James J. Dillon inside a steel cage. The original match scheduled for this show on 10/19 at the Charlotte Coliseum was to be Dusty and Magnum T.A. vs. Ole Anderson and Tully Blanchard. Dillon substituted for Blanchard, who was still on crutches following the injury sustained by Rhodes in Greensboro on 10/11. With Magnum out due to his accident, Dusty

Baby Doll reunited with the Four Horsemen in August of 1986.

"It was only a matter of time before the blonde bomber and the blonde bombshell would walk that aisle together.

- Ric Flair

Photograph by Eddie Cheslock

Pro Wrestling Illustrated / Kappa Publishing

announces on local Charlotte TV on 10/18 that he will have a mystery partner in the match against the Horsemen. That mystery partner turns out to be Nikita Koloff in one of the most memorable, emotional nights in Charlotte wrestling history.

NOVEMBER 1986
The original plans for "Starrcade '86" are changed after Magnum's accident.

Ric Flair successfully defends his NWA World title against Nikita Koloff. Ole and Arn Anderson fail to take the NWA World Tag Team titles from the Rock and Roll Express.

Horsemen Title Change
Tully Blanchard defeats Dusty Rhodes on 11/27 at "Starrcade '86" in Greensboro, NC, for the NWA World TV Championship in a "First Blood" match.

DECEMBER 1986

Dusty Rhodes and Nikita Koloff team against various combinations of the Four Horsemen during the month of December.

Barry Windham enters the area and will play a major role in Horsemen storylines over the next two years.

Small hints of dissension within the Horsemen ranks begin to show themselves. On "World Championship Wrestling" 12/13, Arn says that he was promised a tag team championship, but it hadn't been delivered, and so he plans to win a singles title, targeting Nikita Koloff's United States championship. Arn says he will personally restore the name of Anderson to where it should be. Ole looks a little surprised by the comments. The Horsemen show unity in the end, but it is the first of several small hints over the coming months of Arn asserting his independence from Ole.

Two times on Christmas day, all of the Four Horsemen wrestle as a team in rare 8-man tag matches. Their opponents are Dusty Rhodes, Nikita Koloff, and the Road Warriors, first in Charlotte in the afternoon and then in Atlanta on Christmas night.

As Ole Anderson is talking during an interview on the 12/28 edition of "World Championship Wrestling," J.J. Dillon interrupts him to tell Arn Anderson he thinks he has a contract signed for Arn to wrestle Nikita Koloff for the U.S. title. Ole looks very annoyed.

1987

JANUARY 1987

The month of January features a slow moving series of events that will eventually lead to the first major change in the Four Horsemen:

On the 1/4 Sunday edition of "World Championship Wrestling," Arn Anderson does special commentary with Tony Schiavone during a match with Ole Anderson. Arn is critical of Ole, and it is the first indication of a small split between Ole and the other Horsemen. Arn continues to talk about his embarrassment of not holding a championship and says that will soon change.

On the 1/10 edition of "World Championship Wrestling," Tully Blanchard goes a different direction from Arn the previous week and overly praises Ole Anderson, and is conspicuous in the manner in which he does so.

On the 1/17 edition of "World Championship Wrestling," Lex Luger makes his debut for Jim Crockett Promotions and tells Tony Schiavone that he wants to be a Horseman. Later in the show, the Four Horsemen are interviewed and all indications of trouble between Ole and the other Horsemen seem smoothed over.

On the 1/24 edition of "World Championship Wrestling," Tully Blanchard acknowledges Luger wanting to become a Horseman, but says that there are only four, and James J. Dillon indicates there are no plans for expansion at this time. Later however, after watching him in action, Dillon whispers in the ear of Lex Luger and quickly shakes his hand. Barry Windham confronts his old friend from their "Championship Wrestling from Florida" days and says he doesn't understand why Lex would want to associate with the Horsemen.

On the 1/31/87 edition of "World Championship Wrestling," J.J. Dillon announces that Lex Luger is now officially an "associate" member of the Four Horsemen, but not a full member and there still are no plans to expand. Luger maintains that it his eventual goal to become a Horseman. Later in the show, Lex joins the rest of the Horsemen in a beat-down of Barry Windham and joins in Horsemen unity at the end of the show. However, Ole Anderson, who teamed with Ric Flair earlier in the show, is not present.

Also in January, Barry Windham begins his chase for the World championship. He and Ric Flair have a classic match on 1/20 in Fayetteville, NC, that goes to a time limit draw and is aired in its entirety on the 1/24 edition of "World Wide Wrestling."

FEBRUARY 1987

> *"Lex Luger, you want to be a Horseman? Now's your chance!"*
> *– James J. Dillon*

On 2/4 in Spartanburg, SC, Ric Flair and Barry Windham escalate their feud with a wild brawl at an "NWA Pro Wrestling" taping that would air on 2/7. As Windham begins to get the best of Flair, Tully and Arn hit the ring and the three put a beating on Windham until Dusty Rhodes, Nikita Koloff, and the Armstrongs make the save. With the Horsemen still outnumbered (and Ole Anderson not in the building), Dillon gives Luger a chance to show how he might represent himself as a Horseman. Luger hits the ring and the four fight as a unit, which greatly impresses James J. Dillon.

Lex continues as an associate member of the Four Horsemen throughout the month of February, teaming with various members of the Horsemen, including Ole Anderson.

On the 2/21/87 edition of "World Championship Wrestling," James J. Dillon talks about how not all of the Horsemen can be on TV each and every week, how Ric Flair is not there that week, and how Ole has missed several weeks recently. Ole apologizes for not being able to be there all the time but he has been busy with family obligations, including his son.

Ole then gives a classic interview chronicling the evolution of the Four Horsemen. In a bit of revisionist history, he talks about the original Horsemen being the Anderson family, with Gene, Ole, Arn, and cousin Ric Flair, and when Gene got hurt, the other Horsemen opened their arms to an "outsider" in Tully Blanchard. Ole acknowledges that Lex Luger has come along and wants to be a Horseman.

> *"...And we wrestled all over the world, the best four wrestlers in the world, the Four Horsemen. Until Gene was hurt. And it was at the point for the first time in the history of the Four Horsemen, we took in a man from the outside. We found a man who had all the qualifications and characteristics that were needed to be a Horseman. An outsider, but like one of the family. And I'm talking about the World's Television champion,*

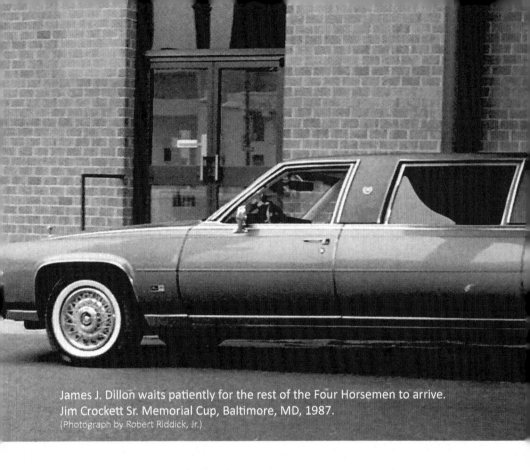

James J. Dillon waits patiently for the rest of the Four Horsemen to arrive. Jim Crockett Sr. Memorial Cup, Baltimore, MD, 1987.
(Photograph by Robert Riddick, Jr.)

> *Tully Blanchard. And right now, we've got another man, we're calling him an associate, he's got all the qualifications that are needed to be a Horseman. But there are only four. I'm talking about Lex Luger, big kid, he's got everything going for him. But there are four Horsemen. Four there are now, four there always will remain. So Lex is going to have to stay an associate for right now."* – Ole Anderson

Dillon raises his eyebrows at Ole's comments on Luger, and the two walk off the set together. Later on in that same show, with Flair absent, the other Horsemen allow Lex to team with them in an 8-man tag match.

The following week, 2/28, James J. Dillon repeats much of what Ole had said the week before about the origins of the Four Horsemen. Tully reminds J.J. that Ole had called him an "outsider" in an earlier interview, and takes exception to that. Ole comes out and asks Tully if there is a problem. When Tully tells Ole that he ought to be spending more time paying attention to the business of the Four Horsemen rather than off

with his "snot-nosed kid," Ole loses his temper and decks Blanchard. J.J. has to separate the two. Later in the show, J.J. comes out and asks Ole Anderson for an apology for hitting Blanchard, and this time Ole slugs Dillon. Tully then attacks him and the two brawl all over the WTBS studio as the credits roll at the end of the show.

A major fracture in the Horsemen has taken place.

MARCH 1987
On the 3/14 edition of "NWA Pro Wrestling," James J. Dillon announces he has made a financial agreement with James E. Cornette for the services of Big Bubba Rogers to eliminate Ole Anderson.

Ole finally speaks on the events that took place two weeks ago. He talks about the importance of family and how he's learned as he's gotten older to not let business come before family. He warns the "outsider" Tully Blanchard and manager James J. Dillon to watch what they say about his kid.

> *"I understand Dillon has got this Big Bubba. Well I tell you what, Bubba, if you think it's easy, ask some of these people here, ask them all around the country what it was like when the Andersons were riding high. I might be an old horse, but as far as I'm concerned, there is still one ride left. ... Arn, you talked about the fire, you looked into my eyes and said maybe the fire was gone. Well you look in my eyes again." – Ole Anderson*

On the 3/14 edition of "World Championship Wrestling," J.J. finally makes it official: Lex Luger is now the fourth Horseman.

On 3/20 in Greensboro, NC, Ole Anderson defeats Big Bubba Rogers in a bounty match. Afterwards, Arn Anderson jumps Ole and he and J.J. Dillon double team Ole and leave him lying in the ring. A few moments later, Ole goes into the Horseman locker room to finally confront Ric Flair and see where he stands on the split in the Horsemen. Flair tells him that it is Ole that turned his back on the team. All of the Horsemen jump Ole and beat him up very badly. The battle lines are now clearly drawn: Ole Anderson now stands alone.

APRIL 1987
At the Jim Crockett, Sr. Memorial Cup in Baltimore, MD, on 4/11, Ric Flair successfully defends the NWA World Championship against Barry Windham. Ole Anderson beats Big Bubba Rogers, and the team of Tully Blanchard and Lex Luger make it to the finals of the tournament only to be defeated by Dusty Rhodes and Nikita Koloff. Arn Anderson and partner Kevin Sullivan (who took Ole's place on the team after his split with the Horsemen) were defeated in an earlier round.

MAY 1987
On the 5/23 edition of "World Championship Wrestling," James J. Dillon talks about how "Tully Blanchard Enterprises" has grown to be larger and more successful than even Exxon and General Motors. He says he promised Tully Blanchard an "executive secretary" a few weeks ago and now he was making good on that promise; he introduces Dark Journey.

On the same show, a video is shown where Dusty Rhodes and Tully Blanchard sign a contract to meet in a "winner take all" battle for $100,000 and the World TV championship. The match will take place on June 6 in Greensboro, NC. Each wrestler must come up with $50,000 on their own, and the winner will take the entire purse and the TV title. All the parties meet in a conference room. Dusty puts up $50,000 in cash of his own money that he brings in a crumpled paper bag. Since Tully is putting up the TV belt, J.J. insists that they receive their normal appearance money in advance, which just happens to be $50,000. Jim Crockett writes the check, J.J. endorses it and, with sly grin, hands it back to Crockett for their share of the $100,000 purse. The TV title that Tully is defending is the championship he won from Dusty in the "First Blood" match the previous November at Starrcade '86.

JUNE 1987
On 6/6 in Greensboro, NC, Tully Blanchard defeats Dusty Rhodes in the $100,000 Winner Take All match, and retains the World TV title in the process. The finish is very controversial. Dusty executes a slingshot suplex on Tully and covers him for the three count. Just after the count, Tully puts his leg over the bottom rope. Referee Tommy Young doesn't see this as it happens, but when he sees Tully's leg moments later, he believes he has incorrectly counted Blanchard out and orders the match to restart. In the meantime, Dark Journey distracts Magnum T.A., who is holding Dusty's share of the winner's purse. J.J. steals the money from Magnum and leaves the building with it. Dusty gives chase to J.J. and as a result is counted out of the ring and loses the match. Tully retain the TV title and wins the $100,000 purse.

After the match, Tommy Young defends his decision, pointing out there is no instant replay in professional wrestling like there is in NFL football. Jim Crockett says there will be a board of inquiry launched to investigate both the match and Mr. Young's refereeing.

Ric Flair later defends Tommy Young, saying he should have told Jim Crockett what he always tells one of his girlfriends when they catch him with another woman: "Honey, are you going to believe me, or your lyin' eyes?"

The Four Horsemen had many battles with Dusty Rhodes and his crew inside the confines of a steel cage match. This one took place at the legendary Greensboro Coliseum in Greensboro, NC. (Photograph by Robert Riddick, Jr.)

On 6/7, the Fabulous Freebirds (Michael Hayes, Terry Gordy, and Buddy Roberts) make their big return to the Omni in Atlanta after many years away only to go down in defeat to Ric Flair, Tully Blanchard, and Lex Luger of the Four Horsemen.

JULY 1987

On July 4th in Atlanta, Dusty Rhodes, Nikita Koloff, the Road Warriors and Paul Ellering defeat the Four Horsemen and James J. Dillon in the first ever "War Games" match. Dillon is legitimately injured in the match by the Road Warriors, separating his shoulder.

Prior to the big show that night at the Omni, James J. Dillon and Paul Ellering have 'warm up matches' on "World Championship Wrestling" on WTBS. Dillon's in particular is a classic, with J.J. executing all four of the Horsemen's signature maneuvers on Alan Martin. The Horsemen lift Dillon high in the air in celebration after the match.

Horsemen Title Change

Lex Luger defeats Nikita Koloff in a cage match for the United States Championship on 7/11 in Greensboro, NC, as part of the Great American Bash tour. James J. Dillon, with his arm in a sling from surgery following his legitimate injury in War Games, pitches a chair over the top of the cage to Luger who nails Nikita with it and knocks him unconscious. Lex then applies the torture rack for the win.

On the same night, Ric Flair defeats Jimmy Garvin to retain the NWA World Heavyweight championship. By virtue of his victory, Flair wins a "dream date" with Garvin's valet, Precious. But Flair doesn't get the date he was anticipating. Ron Garvin shows up dressed in drag and knocks Flair out cold, which would be the first in a series of events that would eventually lead to Ron Garvin challenging Flair for the NWA World title in September.

On 7/31 at the Orange Bowl in Miami, FL, "War Games II" takes place, a rematch from the first War Games at the Bash event in Atlanta on July 4th. This time, The War Machine (Big Bubba Rogers under a mask) takes the place of James J. Dillon who was injured in that first event. Dusty Rhodes, Nikita Koloff, the Road Warriors, and Paul Ellering defeat Ric Flair, Arn Anderson, Tully Blanchard, Lex Luger, and War Machine.

Lex Luger after winning the United States Heavyweight title from Nikita Koloff at the Great American Bash Tour in Greensboro, NC, on July 11, 1987.

(Pro Wrestling Illustrated / Kappa Publishing)

AUGUST 1987
Dark Journey disappears from the scene in early August.

Horsemen Title Change:
Nikita Koloff defeats Tully Blanchard for the World TV title on 8/17 at the TV tapings in Fayetteville, NC.

Ric Flair begins a brutal feud with Ronnie Garvin as Garvin begins his chase of the NWA title.

SEPTEMBER 1987
Horsemen Title Change:
Ron Garvin defeats Ric Flair in a steel cage at Joe Louis Arena in Detroit, MI, on 9/25/87 to win the NWA World Heavyweight championship.

Horsemen Title Change:
Tully Blanchard and Arn Anderson defeat The Rock and Roll Express (Ricky Morton and Robert Gibson) for the NWA World Tag Team championships at a television taping on 9/29/87 in Misenheimer, NC. Eaton and Lane had jumped Ricky Morton earlier and injured his shoulder, and only Robert Gibson was able to come out at first and wrestle in the title match. Eventually Ricky came out when Robert was getting double-teamed and made the tag. Blanchard and Anderson exploited the already injured arm and shoulder but Ricky refused to submit. Eventually Robert waved it off and submitted for the team for fear that his partner would be permanently injured.

OCTOBER 1987
Dusty Rhodes challenges U.S. champion Lex Luger to a match for the title at the upcoming "Starrcade '87" pay-per-view event in Chicago, and asks the legendary Weaver to help him prepare for it by teaching him his famous sleeper-hold. Dusty renames it "the Weaver Lock."

James J. Dillon responds by enlisting the aid of the legendary "Shogun" Hiro Matsuda, master of the Japanese version of the sleeper, to teach Lex to defend against the Weaver Lock and help protect the United States title. Dillon also hopes Matsuda might help him put Dusty Rhodes out of wrestling.

NOVEMBER 1987
Horsemen Title Change
Dusty Rhodes defeats Lex Luger (with James J. Dillon) for the United States championship inside a steel cage on 11/26/87 in Chicago, IL, at Starrcade '87. Just as he had done in July at the Bash in Luger's cage match against Nikita, Dillon threw a chair over the top of the cage but this time it was intercepted by Dusty, who used it to win the title. Johnny Weaver, who taught Rhodes his famous sleeper hold now dubbed "the Weaver lock," was designated as "Keeper of the Key" for the title match in the cage.

"Kampai!" The Horsemen toast Hiro Matsuda.

Horsemen Title Change
Ric Flair defeats Ronnie Garvin in a steel cage on the same Starrcade pay-per-view in Chicago to win the NWA World Heavyweight championship.

Also at Starrcade, Tully Blanchard and Arn Anderson retain their NWA World Tag Team titles against the Road Warriors.

Following Starrcade '87, Arn Anderson expresses disappointment in the fact that not everyone in the Horsemen left Starrcade with gold around their waist, which was a passive-aggressive shot at Lex Luger. Luger looks less than happy with that comment.

Photograph by Robert Riddick, Jr.

Above: Bob Caudle with Arn Anderson and Tully Blanchard at ringside in Greensboro, NC.

At right: United States Champion Lex Luger and James J. Dillon with Tony Schiavone on the set of NWA Pro Wrestling in Spartanburg, SC.

The Horsemen were getting ready for Starrcade '87.

Photograph by Dick Bourne

The "Shogun" Hiro Matsuda was brought in by James J. Dillon in the fall of 1987 to teach Lex Luger the defense for the "Weaver Lock" in preparation for Luger's U.S. title defense against Dusty Rhodes at Starrcade '87.

Matsuda would return in February of 1989 to buy the contracts of the Four Horsemen.

DECEMBER 1987

On 12/2 in Miami, FL, Lex Luger wins the Miami Bunkhouse Stampede and officially splits with the Four Horsemen. (The footage is not shown on television until the weekend of 12/12.)

Before the Miami Stampede, Ric Flair assured Tony Schiavone that there were no problems within the group, but when Schiavone interviewed Lex Luger and James J. Dillon, it was clear that there was indeed a deep division. Luger stated that he knew going into Starrcade that the game plan was flawed (obliquely referring to the chair), a game plan which Dillon had devised for him. Luger told Dillon from now on there would be no further outside interference and that he would win or lose matches on his own.

Luger, Anderson, Blanchard, and Dillon were all entered in the Miami Bunkhouse Stampede. (Flair was not, having defended the NWA World title against Michael Hayes earlier that night.) In the end, it came down to only members of the Horsemen remaining in the ring. Dillon told the referee that they would all split the prize money and share in the victory, but the referee informed him there had to be a single winner. Dillon asked the others if they would let him have this one last victory in his career, to have his name in the record books as a winner of a Bunkhouse Stampede. Arn and Tully immediately agreed and jumped over the top rope and eliminated themselves. But Luger did not. When J.J. got in his face and told him to jump over as well, Luger grabbed Dillon and threw him over the top, thereby winning the Bunkhouse Stampede.

The others jumped Luger at that point and put a classic Horseman-style beating on him, including injuring his right knee.

Arn Anderson speaks for the group:

> "One year ago, J.J. Dillon came to me, came to Flair, came to Tully, and said there is a guy down in the everglades of Florida who has a fantastic body and willing to learn. A diamond in the rough. So what we did was we sacrificed our time to train Luger in the aspects of being a Horseman. He came along real well. Well Luger, for you to stand in the forefront, correct James J. Dillon verbally, then put your hands on him physically,

you put yourself in no-man's land, fella. The Four Horsemen were here long before you came here, and they are going to be here long after you leave. Don't cry about the game plan; the problem was the execution. The game plan was fine, you just weren't the athlete to pull it off." – Arn Anderson

Lex Luger is officially out of the Four Horsemen.

On Christmas night in the Omni, Lex Luger wins the Atlanta Bunkhouse Stampede, and once again is jumped by Arn Anderson and Tully Blanchard (and Dillon, who is at ringside.) Ole Anderson hits the ring to a huge pop (it was Atlanta, after all) and makes the save for Luger. Luger demands a shot at Blanchard and Anderson for the NWA World Tag team titles on New Year's night at the Omni and Ole Anderson agrees to be Luger's partner. The two former Horsemen unite for the one goal of winning the titles.

"Who knows more about the Four Horsemen than the former members of the Four Horsemen? 'The Rock' Ole Anderson and the 'Total Package' Lex Luger - - what a combination."
– Tony Schiavone

Lex and Ole have several matches with Arn and Tully on sequential events at the Omni well into 1988, but ultimately fail to win the tag team titles.

The night after Christmas at a TV taping on 12/26 in Richmond, VA, David Crockett gives Ric Flair a hard time about the Four Horsemen now only being "three Horsemen," but Flair tells him that won't be for long. Flair says "we are taking into consideration Barry Windham" to be a Horsemen and warns Windham that if James J. Dillon brings him a contract, he'd be wise to sign it, as being a Horseman is a once in a lifetime opportunity. It is a tease of what was to come many months later.

1988

JANUARY 1988
Windham is first officially offered the spot as the 4th Horseman on "World Championship Wrestling" on 1/23/88 in a melee following a Western States Heritage title defense, but emphatically turns it down. After the match, Luger apologizes to Windham for the events of a year ago when he joined the Horsemen and the two shake hands and agree to be partners for a big match against Flair and Blanchard in February in Charlotte.

During "Ric Flair Night" in Raleigh's Dorton Arena four days later on 1/26, Sting asks Ric Flair to get in the ring and agree to a NWA World title match. James J. Dillon comes to the ring instead, still holding a glass of champagne from the ongoing celebration taking place. He winds up throwing it in Sting's face, and Sting explodes on J.J. and puts him in scorpion death-lock. Flair and the Horsemen hit the ring to save Dillon, and Flair is so outraged that he agrees to the title match.

FEBRUARY 1988
Valentine's Day was a successful outing for the Horsemen in Atlanta, GA, as Ric Flair successfully defends the NWA World Championship against Sting, and Tully Blanchard and Arn Anderson successfully defend their NWA World Tag Team titles against former Horsemen Ole Anderson and Lex Luger inside a steel cage.

Dusty Rhodes buries the hatchet with both Lex Luger and Ole Anderson, as Dusty reflects on the rich history that he and Ole have at the Omni..

"Through the years we have seen all the champions, everybody on the face of wrestling's earth has been in the Omni in Atlanta. Two men have survived through it all. And when the good Lord gave out guts, he gave Ole Anderson his and a lot of other people's." – Dusty Rhodes

On 2/28 in the Omni, Dusty teamed with Ole Anderson and Lex Luger in a six-man tag match to defeat Ric Flair, Arn Anderson, and Tully Blanchard inside a steel cage. (Armchair booking: wouldn't it have been great if Ole and Lex had turned on Dusty in the cage and re-joined the Horsemen to re-create yet again the angle Dusty had used to such great affect in that same building in 1980 and 1985? Ah, what could have been.)

MARCH 1988
At the WTBS TV taping on 3/21 (airdate 3/26), Dusty Rhodes accidently hits promoter Jim Crockett with a baseball bat while defending Magnum T.A. from an attack by Tully Blanchard at ringside. The NWA launches an investigation.

Horsemen Title Change:
Barry Windham and Lex Luger defeat Tully Blanchard and Arn Anderson for the NWA World Tag Team championships on 3/27/88 at the nationally televised "Clash of the Champions" in Greensboro, NC.

On that same live Clash special, Ric Flair retains the NWA World title in a 45-minute time-limit draw against Sting. Although Sting had been challenging Flair for the title since early February, this was considered Sting's big breakout match as it was seen on national television and went head to head against the WWF's "WrestleMania IV."

APRIL 1988
On the 4/9 episode of "World Championship Wrestling," the NWA Board of Directors strips Dusty Rhodes of the United States championship for the baseball bat incident on 3/21. He is also suspended for 120 days. In defiance of the decision, Rhodes dons a mask and wrestles as the Midnight Rider and is accompanied frequently to the ring by Magnum T.A. If the Midnight Rider is unmasked and revealed to be Dusty Rhodes, Rhodes will receive a lifetime suspension.

Horsemen Title Change
Tully Blanchard and Arn Anderson regain the NWA World Tag Team championships from Barry Windham and Lex Luger on 4/20 in Jacksonville, FL. The match was part of a "World Championship Wrestling" TV taping that aired on 4/23. Windham turns on Luger causing the team to lose the titles, and accepts James J. Dillon's offer to join the Four Horsemen. He even rips the mask from the Midnight

Rider in a dressing room brawl that follows the match, but we are unable to see his identity. As Barry and the rest of the Horsemen ride off in their limousine after the match, a window rolls down and Barry's hands extend through the open window with the mask of the Midnight Rider in one hand and the other hand holding up the four fingers, the sign of the Four Horsemen. It is one of the classic images in Horsemen history.

Barry Windham holds up the four-fingers and the mask of the Midnight Rider.

Windham shows up at the "Jim Crockett Sr. Memorial Cup" in Greensboro, NC, walking the aisle with Ric Flair only hours after his turn has aired on national television. Fans are shocked. Many have not yet seen the turn on television and there are gasps when Barry smiles and slowly holds up the four fingers with Flair.

Sting takes Windham's place as Luger's tag team partner in the tournament, and the two go on to win the Cup, defeating new World Tag Team champions Tully Blanchard and Arn Anderson in the finals. Flair successfully defends the NWA World championship against Nikita Koloff, and James J. Dillon loses to The Midnight Rider (Dusty Rhodes) in a bullrope match.

MAY 1988
On the 5/7 edition of "World Championship Wrestling," David Crockett announces that the suspension of Dusty Rhodes has been lifted and

the NWA board has reinstated him, although the U.S. title will not be returned to him.

Horsemen Title Change
Barry Windham defeats Nikita Koloff on 5/13 in Houston, TX, in the finals of a one-night tournament to fill the vacant United States championship.

Windham begins using the claw-hold as his finisher, wearing a black glove on his right hand. It's a tribute to his father, Blackjack Mulligan, who used the same hold and glove throughout his career.

JUNE 1988
At the 6/8 "Clash of the Champions II: Miami Mayhem" in Miami Beach, FL, the Horsemen retain their titles as Barry Windham defeats Brad Armstrong to retain the United States championship and Arn Anderson and Tully Blanchard successfully defend their World Tag Team titles against Dusty Rhodes and Sting.

At that same show, Ric Flair and Lex Luger sign a contract aboard Bruce McArthur's yacht, the Blackhawk, for an NWA World title match in the main event of the "Great American Bash" pay-per-view event in July.

United States Champion
Barry Windham
(Photograph by Eddie Cheslock)

On the 6/11 editions of "NWA Pro Wrestling" and "World Wide Wrestling" from Savannah, GA, Dusty Rhodes and Barry Windham get into two separate brawls that set up Dusty as the top challenger for Windham's U.S. title.

JULY 1988
At the "Great American Bash: Price for Freedom" pay-per-view in Baltimore, MD, on 7/10, Ric Flair successfully defends the NWA World championship against Lex Luger when the match is controversially stopped by the Maryland State Athletic Commission for blood.

Also at the Bash, Barry Windham defeats Dusty Rhodes to retain the United States championship when Rhodes' friend Ron Garvin turns on him and knocks him out, allowing Barry to win the match.

During the month of July, the Horsemen compete in many War Games events as part of the "Great American Bash Tour" of 1988.

In late July at a TV taping at the Great American Bash event in Columbus, GA, Jim Cornette and the Midnight Express confront James J. Dillon, Arn Anderson, and Tully Blanchard and demand a shot at the NWA World Tag team championships.

SEPTEMBER 1988
Horsemen Title Change
The Midnight Express (Bobby Eaton and Stan Lane with manager Jim Cornette) defeat Tully Blanchard and Arn Anderson for the NWA World Tag team titles on 9/10 in Philadelphia, PA.

Anderson and Blanchard immediately depart for the World Wrestling Federation where they become the "Brain Busters" managed by Bobby Heenan. While Arn Anderson would return in just over a year, Tully Blanchard would never regularly wrestle again for Jim Crockett Promotions or WCW and would never again be a member of the Four Horsemen, although it looked like he might on several occasions.

Photograph by Eddie Cheslock

With the departure of Tully and Arn, the Four Horsemen are now only two Horsemen, still managed by J.J. Dillon and are generally known simply as "the Horsemen" at this point.

OCTOBER 1988
Ric Flair gives an interesting interview on the 10/22 episode of "World Championship Wrestling" where he asks fans to picture the Road Warriors sitting across a table from James J. Dillon and a contract. That reference has fans speculating that the Road Warriors might become Horsemen, although it's likely Flair was simply referencing upcoming matches where he and Barry might team with them. (The Road Warriors had just turned heel on Sting.)

NOVEMBER 1988
Ric Flair teams with Road Warrior Animal vs. Lex Luger and Sting at a Washington D.C. house show. James J. Dillon accompanies Flair and Animal to the ring and Paul Ellering is not with them. Many saw this as part of the same tease that the Road Warriors might become Horsemen.

Barry Windham flashes the sign of a winner (and a champion) after capturing the United States Heavyweight title in a one-night tournament in Houston, TX, on May 13, 1988.

(Pro Wrestling Illustrated / Kappa Publishing)

Jackie Crockett locks his camera tight on NWA World Champion Ric Flair and host Bob Caudle during the opening moments of "NWA Pro Wrestling" in Spartanburg, SC.

Photograph by Dick Bourne

The Legion of Doom and the Four Horsemen

One Saturday in October of 1988, Ric Flair actually teased that the Road Warriors, who had just turned on Dusty Rhodes, might actually become Horsemen.

On the surface, that sounded preposterous. The Four Horsemen were the essence of stylin' and profilin' while Hawk and Animal "snacked on danger and dined on death." Wouldn't it be like mixing oil and water?

Check out this interview Ric Flair did on the October 22 episode of "World Championship Wrestling" and see, if watching and hearing this, you might have thought the same thing:

> "I want you to picture James J. Dillon at a lawyer's desk with a contract for maybe two or three hundred thousand dollars. Then I want you to picture Ric Flair sitting right here, I want you to picture Barry Windham sitting right here, then I want you to picture the Road Warriors at the same table. Think about that; the Road Warriors, God bless them, have finally smartened up. You know what they've done? They've decided to walk on the side of the tracks where the big boys walk. We don't kiss anybody's butts, we do what we want to do anywhere we can do it. And the Road Warriors, I don't like them personally, but as God as my witness, I'll learn to love them. I'll learn to love them like brothers. I'll get women for them,

> *I'll buy them drinks, I'll put them in airplanes, I'll put them in limousines - - all they've got to do is say, "Hey Ric Flair, I want to be your partner." And you know what, Dusty Rhodes, Sting and Luger? It will be, "Jesus; -- Flair, Windham, and the Road Warriors?" How about that, boys? Woooo!"* – Ric Flair

For a moment there, it did seem possible. After all, Arn Anderson and Tully Blanchard had just left for the WWF weeks earlier and fans were curious as to who would fill those slots.

The more likely scenario is that Ric was setting the stage for some upcoming matches where the two teams would simply be joining forces. In fact, Barry Windham did team with the Road Warriors on several occasions in November and December of 1988 against Dusty Rhodes, Sting, and Lex Luger.

But I've got to say, Ric mentioning the LOD at the same table with the Horsemen and a contract in front of them sure made you think - - Animal and Hawk as Horsemen? *Oooooh, what a rush!* ◆

Behind the scenes, the Crockett family sells Jim Crockett Promotions to Atlanta media mogul Ted Turner. The company is renamed "World Championship Wrestling" (WCW).

DECEMBER 1988

Ric Flair and Barry Windham battle The Midnight Express in a dream match at the "Clash of Champion IV: Season's Beatings" on 12/7 in Chattanooga, TN.

Barry Windham teams with the Road Warriors at several house shows (Richmond, Raleigh, Greenville, Winston-Salem, Chicago) against Dusty Rhodes, Sting, and Lex Luger.

At the "Starrcade '88" pay-per-view event in Norfolk, VA, Ric Flair defeats Lex Luger to retain the NWA World Heavyweight championship. Barry Windham defeats Bam Bam Bigelow (with manager Sir Oliver Humperdink) to retain the United States championship.

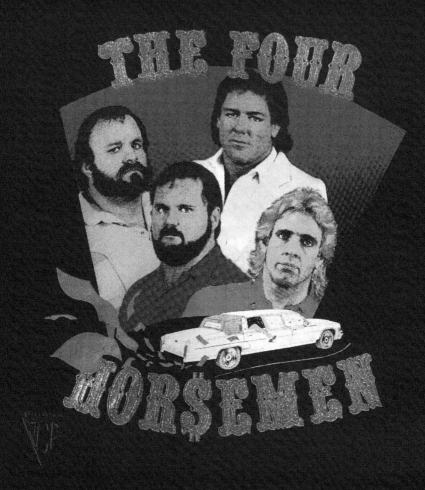

1986 Four Horsemen T-shirt

1987 Four Horsemen T-shirt

Kendall Windham: A Footnote in Horsemen History

There has been much discussion by fans through the years as to whether Kendall Windham was actually a true member of the Four Horsemen. He most definitely was from a technical standpoint, but not so much from a practical standpoint.

Arn Anderson and Tully Blanchard had left for the WWF a few months earlier, leaving two spots to be filled. It appeared Butch Reed might be tapped to fill one of those spots. Barry Windham wanted his brother to fill the other.

Kendall turned heel on his tag-team partner Eddie Gilbert in a match against his brother Barry and Barry's partner James J. Dillon. Afterwards, Dillon raised both men's hands in victory and Kendall held up the four fingers to the fans, letting them know he has just joined the Four Horsemen.

That same weekend in an interview on "World Wide Wrestling," Barry pointed out that by Kendall becoming a member of the Horsemen, he had reunited the Windham family.

But Kendall's tenure as a Horsemen was about to have its legs cut out from underneath it. One week later, Ric Flair and the Windhams introduced Hiro Matsuda as their new manager, whose "Yamazaki Corporation" had purchased the contracts of the Four Horsemen.

Kendall Windham was a Horseman for only one week. But it counts.

He wound up leaving WCW not long after all this happened, and heading back to Florida. ◆

1989

JANUARY 1989

"The American Dream" Dusty Rhodes leaves WCW in mid-January after losing the booking job in December and following the Turner purchase of Jim Crockett Promotions. He opens up Pro Wrestling Federation (PWF) in Florida, and later goes to the WWF.

Butch Reed debuts on the 1/21 Saturday morning edition of "Championship Wrestling" on WTBS and is managed by James J. Dillon. This leads to speculation that Reed is being considered to become part of the Horsemen, and he is considered by some as a loose associate of the Horsemen by virtue of his ties to Dillon. However, that official designation is never given to him, as it was with Lex Luger in early 1987.

Later that same Saturday, Ricky Steamboat debuts in WCW as the mystery partner of Eddie Gilbert and they defeat Ric Flair and Barry Windham in a tag-team match on "World Championship Wrestling."

One week later, Eddie Gilbert hopes to upset the Horsemen again. He takes Kendall Windham (the younger brother of Barry Windham) as his partner and challenges Barry and manager James J. Dillon to a tag team match on the 1/28 episode of "NWA Pro Wrestling." This time the Horsemen gain the upper hand against Gilbert, as Kendall turns and joins his brother and Dillon in putting a Horsemen-style beating on Gilbert. Afterwards, Dillon raises both men's hands in victory and Kendall holds up the four fingers to the fans, letting them know he has just joined the Four Horsemen.

That same weekend in an interview on "World Wide Wrestling," Barry points out that by Kendall becoming a member of the Horsemen, he has reunited the Windham family:

> *"Now that 'K.W.' Kendall Windham is a Horseman, more people are going to stand up and take notice of what we are doing in the ring. Because for the very last time that I'm going to say it, Horsemen are forever, and so are the Windhams."*
> *– Barry Windham*

After Kendall's turn, the Windham brothers become a regular tag-team for a few weeks, managed at first by James J. Dillon. But as the Horsemen struggled to re-build, the rug was pulled out from under them when J.J. Dillon leaves for the WWF.

FEBRUARY 1989
On the Saturday morning "Championship Wrestling" on WTBS on 2/4/89, Ric Flair and the Windhams introduce Hiro Matsuda as their new manager. As the Director of the Yamazaki Corporation, Matsuda announces he has purchased the contracts of the Four Horsemen, and replaces James J. Dillon as the manager of the group.

The timeline shakes out like this: Dillon's last day with WCW is Tuesday 1/31 at the syndicated TV tapings (that air the weekend of 2/4/89.) He manages the Windham brothers as his last official act with the Horsemen on "World Wide Wrestling." The next night 2/1 at the WTBS tapings in Atlanta is when Flair and the Windhams introduce Hiro Matsuda as their new manager. They are now part of Matsuda's Yamazaki Corporation.

As a result of the transition from the Horsemen managed by Dillon to the Yamazaki Corporation managed by Hiro Matsuda, the Four Horsemen as a group go dormant until they are reunited later in the year.

Dillon begins work immediately for the World Wrestling Federation, where he becomes a major player for Vince McMahon behind the scenes for several years before eventually returning to WCW during the Monday Nitro Era. ◆

The beautiful "Big Gold" belt represented the National Wrestling Alliance (NWA) World Heavyweight championship and was held by Ric Flair during most of the Crockett Era of the Horsemen in the 1980s. It would later be recognized as the WCW World title, a championship that Flair won many times throughout the 1990s.

(Photograph by Dick Bourne)

Photographs by Eddie Cheslock

CHAPTER FOUR
Lightening in a Bottle

LOOSE ENDS: THE YAMAZAKI CORPORATION

With the original incarnation of the Four Horsemen coming to an end, we'll take a break from the timeline, tie up some loose ends, and prepare for what is to come.

It is probably fair to say that Hiro Matsuda's stewardship over the former Horsemen was, at best, a disaster. At the "Chi-Town Rumble '89" pay-per-view event in Chicago in February, just weeks after buying the contracts of the Horsemen, both Ric Flair and Barry Windham lost their singles titles on the same night.

Lex Luger defeated Windham for the United States Championship in one of those oddball double-pin situations I've never liked. Windham executed a belly-to-back suplex and held him for the pin. Both men's shoulders were down until right at the count of three when both men got a shoulder up, but referee Tommy Young ruled Luger's was up first, and awarded him the championship. Windham responded by piledriving Luger onto the U.S. title belt.

In a championship match for the ages, Ricky Steamboat defeated Ric Flair for the NWA World Heavyweight title. Referee Tommy Young got knocked down when Steamboat went for the flying body press on Flair. Moments later Flair went for the figure-four, but Steamboat cradled him and a second referee, Teddy Long, came in for the three count and presented the belt to Steamboat. Even though Dusty Rhodes was gone and no longer the booker, it certainly looked as though the "Dusty finish" had stuck around. While lots of fans were expecting the decision to be reversed because the official referee for the match hadn't seen or made the count, Tommy Young surprised everyone, especially Flair and Matsuda, and raised Steamboat's hand, signifying Steamboat was indeed the new world champion.

His stable now void of championships, Mr. Matsuda started scouting Michael Hayes for the Yamazaki Corporation the very next week. In mid-March at the Omni in Atlanta, GA, Hayes turned on tag-team partner Lex Luger in a match against Barry and Kendall Windham (managed by Matsuda) and appeared to have joined the Yamazaki Corporation. The following week, Matsuda made it official. Hayes also joined Jim Ross as the new color commentator for "World Championship Wrestling."

But Hayes joining the Yamazaki Corporation wasn't enough to save it. In late March, Barry Windham left WCW and joined the WWF. Kendall Windham left WCW in early April to work for Dusty Rhodes' PWF promotion in Florida.

Hiro Matsuda would soon disappear from the scene as well. Ironically, his last appearance was at the moment of his lone managerial triumph for the Yamazaki Corporation. Matsuda accompanied Hayes at the "Wrestle War '89" pay-per-view event on May 7 and watched as Hayes defeated Lex Luger for the United States title, albeit with some assistance from the surprise return of Terry Gordy.

From there, the Freebirds were reunited and would pursue tag team titles down the road. Ric Flair regained the NWA World title from Ricky Steamboat and moved on to a long bitter feud

Close, But No Cigar

BUTCH REED

It is very likely that the booking plan in early 1989 was for Butch Reed to become a member of the Four Horsemen, but that plan never had a chance to get off the ground.

"J.J. Dillon is very proud of his newest acquisition. I'm sure he spent some money getting Reed here." – Jim Ross

On Saturday, 1/21/89, "Hacksaw" Butch Reed made his debut in Ted Turner's NWA and was accompanied at ringside by none other than James. J. Dillon. Jim Ross and Tony Schiavone speculated as to the significance of Dillon managing Reed, with the natural assumption being he was under consideration to become a member of the Four Horsemen. After all, the void left months earlier by the departing Arn Anderson and Tully Blanchard made it clear to fans that someone would soon take their place.

We'll never know for sure.

Less than two weeks after Reed's debut, Dillon left for the WWF. The story told was that Hiro Matsuda of the Yamazaki Corporation bought the contracts of Flair, the Windham brothers, and presumably Reed as well. The Horsemen name was dropped altogether and the group was called the Yamazaki Corporation for the next several weeks, managed by Matsuda.

MICHAEL HAYES

While it has occasionally been reported in various sources that Michael Hayes was a Horseman, that is not the case. The confusion stems from Hayes joining Hiro Matsuda's Yamazaki Corporation in March of 1989, not long after Matsuda had purchased the contracts of the Four Horsemen.

One can only imagine, though, that Hayes would have made a terrific addition to the Four Horseman had Dillon not left for the WWF.

Not long after all this, the Yamazaki Corporation dissolved, too. Barry Windham left for the WWF and Ric Flair began focusing on singles feuds with Ricky Steamboat and Terry Funk the rest of 1989. Matsuda was phased out that spring and Reed and Hayes moved on in their own separate storylines. ◆

with Terry Funk. Matsuda quietly vanished, and the Yamazaki Corporation was no more.

By the end of May, any remnants of what were once the Four Horsemen were now completely gone. Ric Flair was the only remaining original member still with the company.

MAJOR BROADCASTER CHANGE

In a move that further illustrates the upheaval within the company at that time, broadcaster Tony Schiavone also left the company for the WWF, going to work as host of their "Wrestling Challenge" television show, along with other responsibilities. Schiavone had been announcing wrestling for Jim Crockett Promotions since 1983 and had been the face and voice of WTBS wrestling programming since 1985. His departure mirrored that of James J. Dillon, with his last work being at the syndicated tapings in Chattanooga, TN, on 1/31. The next night at the WTBS studio tapings for the weekend of 2/4, Jim Ross took over as main host for "World Championship Wrestling," joined by co-host Magnum T.A. Legendary Memphis wrestling broadcaster Lance Russell joined the company and took over as host of "World Wide Wrestling."

LIGHTNING IN A BOTTLE

As is the case with any great movie, it's hard for the sequel to live up to the original. When magic happens for a sports team, it's hard to capture that magic again the following season. There is a reason for that; the original always had something special about it. In the case of the Four Horsemen during the Crockett era, everything was magic. Sometimes the stars just align. Sometimes you catch lightening in a bottle.

That's what happened when the original Four Horsemen came together; it was lightening in a bottle. There was a certain chemistry and camaraderie with the Horsemen over those early years, a chemistry that could never quite be created again.

There were three main problems working against the successful reincarnation of the Four Horsemen. First, there was the ongoing inability to get the originals back together. It wasn't for lack of trying. As we will see as the timeline continues, WCW attempted to bring them all back on two separate occasions in 1989 and 1993, and on both attempts, Tully Blanchard failed to return.

Second, trying to plug other wrestlers into the Four Horsemen proved to be a challenge. There had been almost seamless transitions during the Crockett Era, first from Ole Anderson to Lex Luger, and then from Luger to Barry Windham. In each of those cases, a clear story was well laid out for the transition to make sense and for the fans to buy in. But later, when it was seemingly done without much thought, fans had a hard time getting behind them in the way they had in those early years.

Third, as the 1990s wore on, the Horsemen were no longer booked as the main heel act. The top titles would no longer be theirs as often, and they became fodder for everyone else to kick around.

Another key element that made the Horsemen such a success in the 1980s was gone as well: the camaraderie of the group. They seemingly could never act as a cohesive unit as time went on. I'm not even sure we were really aware of that difference while it was happening. It was sort of a subliminal thing going on that we realized later. The Horsemen never put their hands in together like in the old days, all for one and one for all. It simply wasn't as much fun rooting for the them as they became more and more a dysfunctional unit.

So as we roll towards the first reformation in 1989, we do so with open eyes to the fact that things would never quite be the same again.

Make no mistake; there are some good times ahead. There is some new magic to be made, some special moments to be remembered. But they become far less frequent, and whenever it looks like things might finally get back on track for them, the train derails again.

With every reformation of the Four Horsemen, there is great hope for the magic to return. And with each reformation that falls apart, it is clear you can only catch lightening in a bottle once in a lifetime. ◆

TIMELINE

CHAPTER FIVE
The Early WCW Era
1989-1993

1989

REFORMATION #1
(Sting, Barry Windham, Sid Vicious)

OCTOBER 1989
Ole Anderson returns to WCW on the 10/14 episode of "World Championship Wrestling." Ric Flair and Sting bring out Ole as their surprise 'second' as they prepare to battle Terry Funk and The Great Muta (managed by Gary Hart) in a "Thunderdome" cage at the "Halloween Havoc '89" pay-per-view in Philadelphia, PA on 10/28.

DECEMBER 1989
On the 12/9 edition of "World Championship Wrestling" on WTBS (taped 11/28), Arn Anderson makes his return to the NWA from the WWF, joining Ole Anderson and Ric Flair to reunite the Four Horsemen. They support Flair in his ongoing battle with Gary Hart's J-Tex Corporation

that included The Great Muta and Buzz Sawyer. Behind the scenes, it was supposed to be the reuniting of all four original members of the Horsemen from 1985, but Tully Blanchard's deal with Turner Broadcasting falls through when it is learned that Blanchard failed a drug test just before leaving the WWF.

The Horsemen are fan favorites for the first time, after Ric Flair had turned "good guy" earlier in the year during his battles with Terry Funk over the NWA World title.

Four days after Arn's return on TV, the Horsemen make Sting the new fourth member of the group after Sting defeats Ric Flair in the finals of the Iron Man Tournament at the "Starrcade '89" pay-per-view event on 12/13 in Atlanta, GA. In the spirit of the old saying "Keep your friends close, and your enemies closer," it is part of the Horsemen's plan to prevent Sting from challenging for Flair's NWA World championship. However, when the NWA makes Sting the number one contender and gives him the main event match for the title at the February "Wrestle War" pay-per-view, and Sting doesn't want to turn it down, the Horsemen realize that their plan hasn't worked.

1990

JANUARY 1990
Horsemen Title Change:
Arn Anderson defeats the Great Muta (managed by Gary Hart) to win the World Television title on 1/2 in Gainesville, GA. It was Anderson's second reign as TV champion.

On the 1/27 edition of "World Championship Wrestling," Woman (Nancy Sullivan), who had previously managed the tag team called Doom (Butch Reed and Ron Simmons) begins stalking Ric Flair, interrupting his interviews on occasion, wanting to become his valet. The first incidence of this was when she interrupted Flair during one of Terry Funk's segment's called "Funk's Grill." Flair loved the attention he was getting from Woman, but initially spurned her advances.

Photograph by Eddie Cheslock

FEBRUARY 1990

At the "Clash of Champions X: Texas Shoot-Out" on WTBS on 2/6, the Horsemen announce that since Sting has refused to give up his NWA World title shot against Flair, he is being kicked out of the Four Horsemen.

> *"When you signed that match to meet Ric Flair for the World title on February 25th, you signed your death warrant."*
> *– Ole Anderson*

Ole gives Sting an ultimatum: either back out of the NWA World title match or they will put him out of wrestling that night. When Sting

says not a chance, Flair angrily tells him that he bought him some time because of all Sting had done for him. When Sting grabs Ole to object, the Horsemen pounce and leave Sting lying in the ring.

Later as the Horsemen battled Gary Hart's J-Tex Corporation in a six-man cage match, Sting charged the ring but badly injured his knee (legit) when trying to climb the cage to get at Flair. The injury and resulting reconstructive surgery put Sting on the shelf for about 5 months, knocking him out of his NWA title match with Flair after all.

Woman starts officially accompanying Ric Flair and the Horsemen on the 2/10/90 episode of "World Championship Wrestling."

Lex Luger takes Sting's place in the NWA world title match at the "Wrestle War '90: Wild Thing" pay-per-view on 2/25 in Greensboro, NC, but fails to take the title away from Flair.

Also at "Wrestle War," Rick and Scott Steiner successfully defend the WCW World Tag Team titles against Ole and Arn Anderson. Arn injures his neck (legit) on this show and is out of action for several months, although he continues to appear with the Horsemen in TV interviews. (It would be this injury that eventually leads to Arn's retirement several years later.)

MARCH 1990

With Arn temporarily out of action, Ole Anderson begins managing a new masked tag team for several months that he calls 'Minnesota Wrecking Crew II' (Wayne Bloom and Mike Enos

from the AWA) to continue the feud with the Steiner Brothers. The Wrecking Crew, although managed by Ole, are not affiliated with the Horsemen.

APRIL 1990
Barry Windham makes a surprise return to WCW at the 4/23 syndicated TV tapings in Marietta, GA. It airs on the 5/9 edition of "World Wide Wrestling." He does a run-in to assist NWA Champion Ric Flair during a title defense against Lex Luger.

Windham rejoins the Four Horsemen, which now consists of Ole and Arn Anderson, Ric Flair and Barry Windham, with Woman in tow as a valet, primarily to Flair.

Around this same time, Ole Anderson retires from in-ring wrestling and effectively becomes the manager of the Four Horsemen.

MAY 1990
During one of Jim Cornette's "Louisville Slugger" segments on the 5/11 Friday night episode of "WCW Power Hour," Sid Vicious is introduced as the newest member of the Four Horsemen. Ric Flair and Ole Anderson are Cornette's guests, and they use the platform of the Slugger to introduce Sid as the newest member. Sid is escorted to the ring by Woman. The "Capitol Combat" pay-per-view event in Washington D.C. is just two days later.

Not long after Sid joins the Horsemen, Woman leaves the group.

The Four Horsemen are now officially at full strength again and include Ric Flair, Arn Anderson, Barry Windham, and Sid Vicious, managed by Ole Anderson. (Arn remains out of action awhile longer, though, due to the injury he sustained against the Steiner brothers.)

< Facing page: A magazine spread and article featuring the newly re-formed Four Horsemen in 1990.

At "Capitol Combat" on 5/19 in Washington, DC, Ric Flair again retains the NWA World championship against Lex Luger in a steel cage match when Ole Anderson has the cage lifted up far enough for Barry Windham to enter and interfere.

JUNE 1990
At the "Clash of the Champions XI - Coastal Crush" on 6/13 in Charleston, SC, the Horsemen have several singles matches: Barry Windham defeats Doug Furnas, Sid Vicious loses to Lex Luger, and Ric Flair loses to Junkyard Dog by DQ when the other Horsemen interfere. Arn Anderson returns to action in a losing effort to Paul Orndorff.

JULY 1990
Sting, making a triumphant return to action after his knee injury in February, defeats Ric Flair for the NWA World Heavyweight title at "The Great American Bash" pay-per-event on 7/7 in Baltimore, MD. It is thought at that moment to be the passing of the torch to Sting, who is seen as the face of WCW going forward. That would wind up not entirely being the case.

Also on this Bash show, the "Dudes with Attitudes" (Paul Orndorff, Junkyard Dog, and El Gigante) defeat Arn Anderson, Barry Windham, and Sid Vicious by D.Q.

During the NWA World title match, Ole Anderson is handcuffed to El Gigante to prevent Ole from interfering. Not long after the Bash, Ole Anderson disappears from the scene, but is still involved behind the scenes booking for WCW.

At some point after the Great American Bash, the company renames its championship the WCW World Heavyweight title, dropping the NWA recognition.

Ric Flair suffers a legit knee injury a week after the "Great American Bash" and is out of action for a couple of weeks. Former NWA World champion Harley Race replaces him in several Horsemen tag matches.

At the TV taping on 7/16 in Gainesville, GA, Lex Luger is attacked off-camera in the parking lot, and it is later revealed that the Horsemen were the perpetrators.

SEPTEMBER 1990

At the "Clash of the Champions XII: Mountain Madness" event (also subtitled "Fall Brawl '90") on 9/5 in Asheville, NC, Ric Flair challenges Lex Luger for the WCW United States championship. This was set up by the parking lot attack on Luger in Gainesville back in July. Flair was anxious to work his way back into the world title picture and the U.S. title is thought to be the stepping-stone. He had previously held that title for a record five times. Stan Hansen attacked Luger during the match causing Flair to get disqualified, although Hansen wasn't there to help Flair. He was also upset about his standing in the WCW rankings and wanted a shot at Luger's U.S. title, which he would receive and would win the title at the next pay-per-view event.

OCTOBER 1990

At the "Halloween Havoc '90" pay-per-view event on 10/27 in Chicago, IL, Ric Flair and Arn Anderson fail to win the WCW World Tag Team championships from Doom (Ron Simmons and Butch Reed managed by Teddy Long) when both teams were counted out of the ring.

Also on that same Halloween Havoc show, Sid Vicious challenges Sting for the WCW World Heavyweight championship that features one of the most bizarre attempts to steal the world title the Horsemen had ever devised. During the match, Sid actually leaves the ring area with Sting in hot pursuit while Ric Flair and Arn Anderson distract referee Nick Patrick at ringside. Moments later Sid and Sting return to the ring. Sting goes for a bodyslam but Sid falls on top of him for the surprising three count. He is announced as the new WCW World champion and given the belt as the fireworks go off and orange and black balloons drop from the ceiling. Suddenly Sting is back in the ring with ropes hanging from his wrists as if he had been tied up. The referee, without explanation, restarts the match. Sting grabs the big gold belt, whacks Sid in the head with it, delivers a Stinger splash and cradles Sid for the three-count.

The Four Horsemen, The Black Scorpion, and Barry Windham's Grand Deception

The Black Scorpion was a mysterious character that tormented Sting during the fall of 1990. There were several connections between the Scorpion and the Horsemen, not the least of which was that the Scorpion's secret identity was eventually revealed to be Ric Flair at Starrcade.

The haunting voice of the Scorpion heard throughout the arenas leading up to Sting's match with Ric Flair at Starrcade was none other than that of Ole Anderson.

But it was perhaps Barry Windham's connection to the Black Scorpion that was the strangest of all. In one of wrestling's most memorable trick-or-treat moments, Windham assumed the identity of the 'fake Sting' that entered the ring at Halloween Havoc and allowed fellow-Horseman Sid Vicious to pin him, which momentarily had Sid thinking he had won the WCW World title. The plot was said to be a concoction of the Black Scorpion. ◆

Sting is then announced as champion and given the belt. Needless to say, confusion reigned at the live event. It turns out that when Sting originally chased Sid to the back, he was apparently restrained and a fake-Sting returned to the ring and it was this fake-Sting that was pinned by Sid. That fake-Sting turned out to be none other than Barry Windham with a new haircut and made up to look remarkably like Sting in an attempt to steal the title. It isn't clear how the referee figured it out so quickly, but he did, and the title stayed with its rightful owner.

NOVEMBER 1990
At the "Clash of the Champions XIII: Thanksgiving Thunder" event on 11/20 in Jacksonville, FL, Ric Flair defeats Butch Reed, and by doing so earns a World Tag Team title rematch for the Horsemen with Doom after their Halloween Havoc match had resulted in double count out. Flair also wins the services of Doom's manager Teddy Long as his chauffeur-for-a-day by virtue of a side-wager with Long. Arn Anderson is at ringside with Flair, while Ron Simmons had accompanied Reed.

On the same Clash event, Sid Vicious defeats the Night Stalker.

DECEMBER 1990
Horsemen Title Change:
The Z-Man (Tom Zenk) defeats Arn Anderson for the WCW World Television championship on 12/4 in Gainesville, GA.

At the "Starrcade '90: Collision Course" pay-per-view event on 12/16 from the historic Kiel Auditorium in St. Louis, MO, Sting defeats the Black Scorpion to successfully defend the WCW World championship. The Black Scorpion is unmasked and revealed to be none other than Ric Flair, who now along with Barry Windham is also sporting a much shorter haircut.

On the same Starrcade card, Barry Windham and Arn Anderson fail to take the WCW World Tag Team titles away from Doom (Ron Simmons and Butch Reed.)

1991

JANUARY 1991

Horsemen Title Change
Ric Flair regains the WCW World Heavyweight championship from Sting on 1/11 at the Meadowlands in East Rutherford, NJ. Flair, who looked to be completely out of the world title picture as little as a month earlier, is back on top of the wrestling world again.

Horsemen Title Change
Arn Anderson regains the WCW World Television title on 1/14 in Marietta, GA.

After the Horsemen had failed to take the World Tag Team titles from Doom at "Halloween Havoc" and "Starrcade," Barry Windham and Arn Anderson get "back to the basics" in two memorable black-and-white vignettes where they visit some pretty rough neighborhoods, smashing cars with sledgehammers, and predicting "Armageddon." They set a new tone for the Horsemen in 1991.

At the "Clash of the Champions XIV: Dixie Dynamite" on 1/30 in Gainesville, GA, Sid Vicious defeats Joey Maggs, Arn Anderson and Barry

Windham defeat The Renegade Warriors (Chris Youngblood and Mark Youngblood), and Ric Flair fights Scott Steiner to a draw when TV time expired to successfully defend the WCW World championship.

FEBRUARY 1991

At the "Wrestle War '91" pay-per-view event on 2/24 in Phoenix, AZ, a special War Games match is held. It features the team of Sting, Brian Pillman, and the Steiner Brothers against three of the Four Horsemen (Ric Flair, Sid Vicious, and Barry Windham) and their partner Larry Zbyszko, who replaces an injured (legit) Arn Anderson. Sting's team wins when Pillman is knocked unconscious by a Sid Vicious power-bomb and El Gigante submits for him from the outside of the War Games cage.

MARCH 1991

Tatsumi Fujinami defeats Ric Flair at the huge "Starrcade at Tokyo Dome" event on 3/21 at the Tokyo Dome in Tokyo, Japan. The event is a co-promotion of New Japan Pro Wrestling and World Championship Wrestling. The match is billed in Japan as for the NWA World Heavyweight title because that name meant much more there than the WCW name did. Because of controversy surrounding the finish and who was the official referee making the count, WCW returns the title belt to Ric Flair. However, the NWA recognizes Fujinami's win. While never explained fully as such to U.S. audiences, the two are scheduled to meet again at the inaugural "Superbrawl" event in the U.S. in May to resolve the title situation.

MAY 1991

Horsemen Title Change
Arn Anderson loses the WCW TV title to Bobby Eaton on 5/19 at the inaugural "Superbrawl" pay-per-view event in St. Petersburg, FL.

Ric Flair defeats Tatsumi Fujinami in the main event of that same show, putting to rest the dispute over who was recognized as the WCW World Heavyweight Champion. Fujinami defeated Flair at the Tokyo Dome in Japan two months earlier and was briefly recognized as NWA champion there, while Flair retained recognition as WCW champion in the United States. Flair's win at Superbrawl ended that controversy.

The Horsemen basically dissolve soon after Superbrawl in May. Sid Vicious' contract with WCW expires and he leaves for the WWF. Barry Windham declares on TV that he is going after any and all titles, and that includes the WCW World title held by Ric Flair. Of course, Flair would also leave the promotion in July, fired by WCW and eventually making the jump to the WWF, a move that has been somewhat anticipated since late 1988. The real surprise in that move is that Flair takes the WCW "big gold" world title belt with him and is actually recognized as the "real world champion" in the WWF. After Flair leaves WCW, Arn Anderson forms a tag team with Larry Zbyszko dubbed "The Enforcers" and they go on to win the WCW World Tag Team championships and join the new stable of Paul E. Dangerously's "Dangerous Alliance" in November of 1991. Ole Anderson begins work solely behind the scenes after the Great American Bash in July.

The first reformation of the Four Horsemen in the Early WCW Era had now come to an end.

1993

REFORMATION #2
(Paul Roma)

FEBRUARY 1993
Ric Flair returns to WCW after a two-year run in the World Wrestling Federation that included two reigns as WWF Champion. His first appearance back with the company is at the "Superbrawl III" pay-per-view event on 2/21 in Asheville, NC. He presents the "big gold" title belt, once again representing the NWA World Heavyweight championship, to Barry Windham after Windham defeats the Great Muta for the title. Windham and Flair have a stare-down in the ring and the tension is thick as we anticipate that Flair may want to challenge Windham in an attempt to regain the title he never lost when he left the company in 1991.

Flair is unable to compete in WCW for a few months because of the no-compete clause in his contract with the WWF. During that time, he hosts a weekly television segment called "A Flair for the Gold" and is joined on the set each week by his former partner Arn Anderson. Arn starts pushing Flair to get the Four Horsemen back together.

MAY 1993
The second reformation of the Four Horsemen in the 'Early WCW Era' takes place during a segment of "A Flair for the Gold" at the inaugural Slamboree pay-per-view event on 5/23 in Atlanta, GA. Ole Anderson

returns for one night only with the original plan to reunite the original four members (Flair, Arn, Ole, and Tully Blanchard) for what was billed as a "Horsemen Reunion." However, Paul Roma appears as the new 4th Horseman in place of Blanchard, when Blanchard and WCW could not agree to contract terms. (Ole was also there that night to be inducted into the WCW Hall of Fame.) In the storyline, NWA World champion Barry Windham is blamed for talking Tully Blanchard out of rejoining the Horsemen.

The segment is still billed and promoted as the reunion of all four original Horsemen, even though WCW knows Tully Blanchard will not appear well in advance. When Roma is announced as the fourth Horseman, the reaction by fans is less than welcoming.

While the first reformation of the Horsemen in 1990 with Barry Windham and Sid Vicious would be labeled a success, this second reformation in 1993 would never really get off the ground. With Ole only there for the big night at Slamboree, it was really just the 'three Horsemen' after Slamboree. Flair remains in singles programs with Barry Windham and Rick Rude over the NWA world title, while Anderson and Roma form a tag team and go on to win the WCW World Tag Team titles. But fans never really accept that the Horsemen are back together at all, even though the promotion continues to push them as the Horsemen for months.

On that same Slamboree card, Arn Anderson challenges reigning NWA World Champion (and former Horseman) Barry Windham for the title, but fails to win the "big gold" belt.

AUGUST 1993
Horsemen Title Change
Arn Anderson and Paul Roma defeat Steve Austin and Lord Steven Regal (substituting for an injured Brian Pillman) to win the NWA World Tag team championships on 8/18 in Daytona, FL. During their title reign, WCW withdraws from the NWA and Anderson and Pillman are recognized as WCW World Tag Team champions from that point forward.

SEPTEMBER 1993
Horsemen Title Change
The Nasty Boys (Brian Knobs and Jerry Saggs) defeat Arn Anderson and Paul Roma for the WCW World Tag Team titles on 9/19 at the Fall Brawl '93 pay-per-view event in Houston, TX.

OCTOBER/NOVEMBER 1993
At the TV tapings in Dalton, GA, Arn Anderson wrestles Paul Orndorff (managed by the Assassin) in a singles match. Steve Austin hits the ring and he and Orndorff double team Arn until Paul Roma belatedly makes

the save. Arn looks at Roma as if to ask "what took you so long?" This sets up a tag team match the following week between Arn and Paul Roma vs. Austin and Orndorff. In that tag match, Arn is repeatedly double-teamed and Roma refuses to tag in, apparently at the direction of the Assassin. Roma subsequently turns heel and forms a tag team with Orndorff called "Pretty Wonderful" managed by the Assassin (Jody Hamilton.)

Arn Anderson and Sid Vicious get into a legit fight while on a WCW tour of England where both men are seriously wounded. Sid winds up getting fired, but Anderson is retained, although he is out of action for two months.

DECEMBER 1993
Horsemen Title Change
Ric Flair defeats Vader to win the WCW World Heavyweight Championship on 12/27 at the Starrcade '93 pay-per-view event in Charlotte, NC. Flair was put back into the title picture replacing Sid Vicious in this match when Vicious was fired after the altercation with Arn Anderson in England. It is a major personal vindication for Flair, who once again rides atop the company as champion, although that company is in major disarray at this point in time.

Arn Anderson returns to action after Christmas following recuperation from injuries sustained in the altercation with Sid Vicious. He defeats his former partner Paul Roma in a singles match on television and puts an end to the sad history of Paul Roma as Horsemen.

As 1993 draws to a close with Arn just getting back to singles action, Roma turning heel and now teaming with Paul Orndorff, and Ric Flair now once again World champion, the second reformation of the Four Horsemen in the "Early WCW Era" has fizzled out without anyone really even noticing. It is a sad state of affairs for a faction that is considered the greatest ever. But like a phoenix rising from the ashes, 1995 will see Ric Flair and Arn Anderson once again revive the Horsemen as we enter the "Monday Nitro Era." ◆

TIMELINE

CHAPTER SIX
The Monday Nitro Era
1995-1999

1995

REFORMATION #3
(Brian Pillman, Chris Benoit, Steve McMichael, Jeff Jarrett, Curt Hennig)

AUGUST 1995
The story of the 1995 reformation of the Horsemen actually begins with a major rift between two of its founding members. Following a loss to Vader in a handicap tag-team match, Ric Flair and Arn Anderson have a falling out and the unthinkable happens: they schedule a one-on-one match against each other at Fall Brawl.

SEPTEMBER 1995
In the build-up to their match on 9/17 at the "Fall Brawl '95" pay-per-view event in Asheville, NC, Arn takes the highroad while Flair lives up to

his reputation as "the dirtiest player in the game." But when the match finally takes place, it is Flair who fights Anderson cleanly, and Arn who uses the help from his friend Brian Pillman to defeat Flair in the historic match-up.

Arn Anderson and Brian Pillman declare themselves the "New Horsemen" and vow to put Flair out of wrestling. But it would all prove to be a giant swerve.

OCTOBER 1995
Ric Flair talks U.S. champion Sting into taking him as his partner to battle Anderson and Pillman in matches on Nitro on 10/16 and at "Halloween Havoc" on 10/29. Sting has finally developed a level of trust in the Nature Boy, but in classic Horseman style, Flair turns on Sting in a move apparently everyone except Sting saw coming, although to be fair to the Stinger, he had his doubts all along and perhaps should have trusted his first instincts.

With Flair and Arn reuniting and taking Pillman on as a third horseman, the newest reformation of the Horsemen is underway.

NOVEMBER 1995
The third Horsemen reformation is completed as Flair, Anderson, and Pillman, are joined by "The Crippler" Chris Benoit to round out the "New Breed" of the Four Horsemen.

DECEMBER 1995
Horsemen Title Change
At "Starrcade '95" at the Municipal Auditorium in Nashville, TN, on 12/27, a "Triangle Match" is set up between Ric Flair, Lex Luger, and Sting to determine a number one challenger for Randy Savage's WCW World championship. The winner of the triangle match would get the title match with Savage that same night. Flair defeats Sting and Luger by count-out, and then with the help of the Four Horsemen (and even an assist by Jimmy Hart) defeats Savage to win yet another in his long string of World championships.

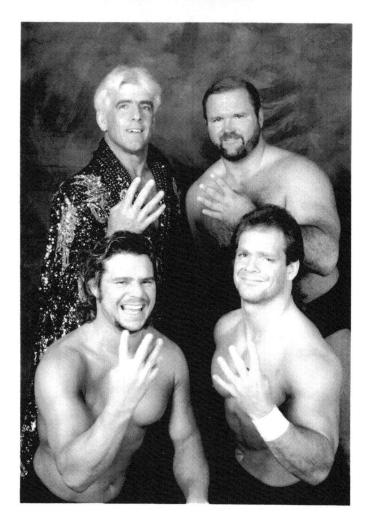

Promotional photograph purchased at a WCW arena house show in the 1990s.

1996

JANUARY 1996

A special New Year's Night edition of "WCW Monday Nitro" from Atlanta, GA, features two big main events showcasing the Horsemen. First Randy Savage gets a matter of revenge on Arn Anderson by hitting him with brass knuckles to win their contest. Just a few days earlier, Arn had hit Savage with a pair of knucks to help Ric Flair win the WCW World title.

> *"Baby, I told the wrestling world that if I got back in the ballgame, I wouldn't just play, I'd win."*
> *— Ric Flair*

In the main event of this same Nitro, Flair defends that newly won world title against Hulk Hogan and retains the title by disqualification.

Jimmy Hart, who is primarily aligned with The Giant, accompanies Ric Flair during his matches during the entire month of January. He is never considered affiliated with the Horsemen; it is more of a political alliance to aid The Giant in his battles with Hulk Hogan and Randy Savage.

Horsemen Title Change
On the 1/22 edition of "Monday Nitro," Randy Savage regains the WCW World title from Ric Flair when Arn Anderson tries to hit the Hulkster with brass-knucks but hits Ric Flair by mistake.

FEBRUARY 1996

On the 2/5 edition of "Monday Nitro," Woman turns on Randy Savage during a match with Chris Benoit and aligns herself with the Four Horsemen. Woman has been part of a group of women, including Miss Elizabeth and Debra McMichael, that accompany Randy Savage and Hulk Hogan.

Horsemen Title Change
Ric Flair defeats Randy Savage for the WCW World Heavyweight championship at Superbrawl VI on 2/11/96 at the Bayfront Arena in

St. Petersburg, FL. Savage's longtime valet Miss Elizabeth turns on him to help Flair win the title by giving Flair one of her high-heeled shoes, which he uses as a foreign object to defeat Savage. She then becomes a valet to the Horsemen.

On that same pay-per-view, Brian Pillman (who wins the award for the most volatile personality to ever be in the Four Horsemen) bails out of the ring during a "Respect" strap match with Kevin Sullivan in the infamous "I Respect you, booker man" incident. Pillman has been involved in a bizarre work/shoot with WCW booker Kevin Sullivan for months which partially plays out right on live television. In the end it was a work on the boys themselves, and Pillman used it to eventually gain a contractual release from WCW. Pillman leaves the company (and the Horsemen) and goes to work for the rival WWF in the heat of the Monday night wars.

APRIL 1996
Horsemen Title Change
The Giant (Paul Wight, later known in the WWE as The Big Show), managed by Jimmy Hart, defeats Ric Flair for the WCW world title on 4/22 at "Monday Nitro" in Albany, GA.

JUNE 1996
"WCW Monday Nitro" co-host (and former legendary Super Bowl-winning defensive tackle for the Chicago Bears) Steve "Mongo" McMichael decides to leave the commentary desk and team up with fellow NFL star Kevin Greene in a tag-team match against Ric Flair and Arn Anderson at the "Great American Bash" pay-per-view event on 6/16 in Baltimore, MD. The match comes about because of Ric Flair's flirtation with Mongo's wife Debra McMichael, which enrages Mongo enough for him to decide to settle it with Flair in the ring. He enlists the aid of current NFL superstar Kevin Greene (an all-pro linebacker for the Carolina Panthers) to go against the Horsemen. McMichael and Greene enlist Randy Savage to second them. Bobby Heenan serves as "Coach" to Flair and Anderson leading up to the match, and they are also accompanied by Miss Elizabeth and Woman.

But it is all another classic Horsemen swerve. Mongo turns on Greene, hitting him over the head with a Halliburton briefcase containing a Horsemen t-shirt and a whole lot of cash, and Mongo becomes the new fourth Horsemen.

The "Great American Bash" show is a great night for the Four Horsemen. Not only does Mongo join the ranks, but there is a classic moment of unity for Arn Anderson and Chris Benoit as well. This is during a time when Kevin Sullivan, who has been a close friend of Arn's in the past, is trying to drive a wedge into the Horseman and it looks like it is working. After Benoit beats Sullivan in a "falls count anywhere" match at the Bash, he continues to put the boots to the "Games Master." Sullivan's manager Jimmy Hart begs Arn to assist his old friend Sullivan, and when Arn first hits the ring, he indeed pulls Benoit off Sullivan. It looks as though Arn will side with Sullivan, but instead both he and Benoit put the boots to him, which garners one of the biggest pops of the night from the crowd.

The Horsemen are completely united coming out of the "Great American Bash."

JULY 1996
Horsemen Title Change
Ric Flair defeats Konnan to win the WCW United States championship on 7/7 in Daytona Beach, FL, at the "Bash at the Beach" pay-per-view event. For old school fans of Flair, this was an interesting title win. The WCW United States championship has direct lineage back to the U.S. title that originated in Jim Crockett Promotions in 1975. It was a title that Flair held on five different occasions between 1977 and 1981, trading it with such stars as Bobo Brazil, Ricky Steamboat, Jimmy Snuka, and Roddy Piper. Now just over 15 years after last losing that title in January of 1981, Flair wins this historic championship for an unprecedented sixth time.

SEPTEMBER 1996
Ric Flair is injured in a match against Kensuke Sasaki in Japan on 9/21. The legitimate shoulder injury requires Flair to forfeit the WCW U.S. title

and will keep him out of action for several months, although he will continue to accompany the Horsemen during that down time.

By the end of September, Miss Elizabeth begins to distance herself from the Four Horsemen, as she is involved in a storyline with Randy Savage and the nWo. This follows an incident at the "Fall Brawl" pay-per-view event on 9/15 where she was attacked and spray-painted by the nWo when trying to defend Savage from an nWo assault. After the 9/30 Nitro, where Arn Anderson and Woman confront her over this, she basically is no longer associated with the Horsemen.

Chris Benoit and Woman start a personal relationship that becomes a disruption and distraction within Four Horsemen, and creates tension with Kevin Sullivan (Woman's husband) and his stable, the Dungeon of Doom.

OCTOBER 1996
Jeff Jarrett makes his WCW Monday Nitro debut on 10/7 and defeats Hugh Morris. With Flair unable to compete due to his legit injury back in September, he endorses Jarrett as an "honorary" Horseman and asks him to be his replacement in his match at the 10/27 "Halloween Havoc" Pay-per-view event against the Giant. The rest of the Horsmen are less than pleased with this. With Flair out of action following surgery over the next several months, Jarrett lobbies to become an official member of the Horsemen, but Flair is seemingly the only one early on that wants him.

DECEMBER 1996
Jeff Jarrett's ongoing desire to become a Horseman and Chris Benoit's ongoing desire to be with Woman continue to create conflict within the group. Ric Flair continues his endorsement of Jarrett, and Arn is caught in the middle. However, Arn shows his hand when he sides with Benoit in his "Starrcade '96" match with Jarrett on 12/29 in Nashville, TN, a match Jarrett wins with the help of Kevin Sullivan.

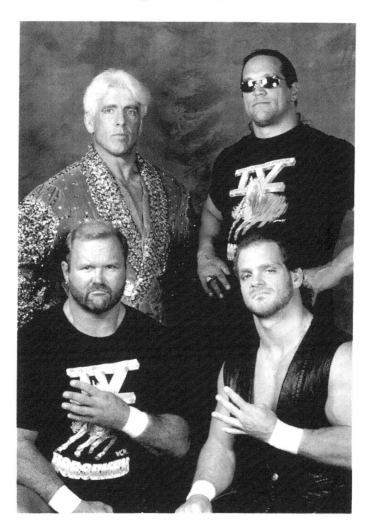

Promotional photograph purchased at a WCW arena house show in the 1990s.

1997

FEBRUARY 1997

Jeff Jarrett defeats Steve McMichael on 2/23 at the "Superbrawl VII" pay-per-view event at the Cow Palace in San Francisco, CA, and by virtue of the win becomes a member of the Four Horsemen. Ric Flair had agreed two days earlier on "WCW Saturday Night" on Superstation WTBS that if Jarrett beat Mongo, he could join the group, although no one else in the group (except Mongo's wife Debra) seemed to be high on the idea.

The next night 2/24 on "Monday Nitro" in Sacramento, CA, Flair and Arn Anderson force McMichael and Jarrett to put aside their differences and shake hands. Mongo, the better man, steps up and puts his hard feelings aside:

"I never said you wasn't family, my brother. I might mess with you, but nobody else better. Here's my hand."
– Steve McMichael to Jeff Jarrett

The two shake hands. For the first time, Jarrett holds up the four-fingers with the rest of the group and is officially accepted as a Horseman. But despite getting what he wants, Jarrett is a source of disruption for the Horsemen over the next four months, constantly at odds with partner Steve McMichael.

MARCH 1997

Roddy Piper enlists the aid of the Horsemen (Benoit, Jarrett, and McMichael) to form a team to battle the nWo (Hogan, Hall, Nash, and Savage) and WCW (Luger, Scott Steiner, and The Giant) in a triangle elimination match at the "Uncensored" pay-per-view event on 3/16 in North Charleston, SC. The match was won by the nWo team.

JUNE 1997

Horsemen Title Change

Jeff Jarrett (with Queen Debra) defeats Dean Malenko to win the United States championship on 6/9 in Boston, MA on "Monday Nitro." Jarrett gets an assist from a returning Eddie Guerrero, who executes a frog-splash on Malenko while Debra distracts the referee.

At the "Great American Bash" pay-per-view event on 6/15 in Moline, IL, NFL star Kevin Greene defeats Steve McMichael when Jeff Jarrett accidentally hits Mongo with the Halliburton briefcase when he had intended to hit Greene. It appears to be an honest mistake, but this miscue causes Ric Flair to place Jarrett on "probation" from the Four Horsemen.

Two weeks later on the 6/30 "Monday Nitro" from Las Vegas, NV, Flair interferes to help Jarrett defeat Konnan to retain the U.S. title, and it appears that all is forgiven for the transgression at the Bash and that Jarrett might soon be off probation. Flair and Jarrett even do the strut together in the ring after the match. However, when the other Horsemen join them, Flair tells Jarrett that "familiarity breeds contempt" and that Jarrett is being kicked out of the Horsemen. Jarrett protests, telling Flair they are all jealous of his success, but Flair shrugs it off. Mocking Jarrett's country-guitar gimmick, Flair says to him:

> *"Tell your story walkin', Alan Jackson. You're out."*
> *- Ric Flair*

JULY 1997

Following his surprise debut in the closing seconds of "Monday Nitro" a week earlier, Curt Hennig announces on the 6/7 episode of "Monday Nitro" that his services are available to the group that makes him the best offer.

> *"As of right now, Curt Hennig is a free agent, and I don't want anybody in the back room to take the word 'free' lightly."*
> *— Curt Hennig*

Ric Flair embraces Hennig and announces that Hennig is there to join the Four Horsemen, but Hennig tells Flair not to jump to conclusions. The nWo is also interested in Hennig.

At the "Bash at the Beach" pay-per-view on 7/13 in Daytona Beach, FL, Jeff Jarrett defeats Steve McMichael to retain the U.S. title. Debra McMichael turns on her husband in this match. She leaves Mongo to accompany Jarrett as his valet from this point forward. As Debra has been the root of all the disharmony within the Horsemen over the last year, the group is much better off without her. And although he might not know it at the time, Mongo is, too.

Ric Flair continues to recruit Curt Hennig to join the Four Horsemen, and even teams with him on the 7/28 "Monday Nitro," but Hennig remains very non-committal about joining the group. He is even seen helping the New World Order (nWo) on occasion with some of their monkey business.

AUGUST 1997

Horsemen Title Change
Steve "Mongo" McMichael defeats Jeff Jarrett (with Queen Debra) to win the U.S. title on 8/2 in Nashville, TN at what would be the final "Clash of the Champions" special on WTBS, a series which began back in 1988. Mongo won when Eddie Guerrero interfered intending to hit Mongo with the U.S. belt, but instead hit Jarrett. When McMichael covered him for the three-count, the crowd popped big to finally see Mongo get his revenge on Jarrett and his soon-to-be-ex-wife, Debra.

Later, on the same "Clash of the Champions" special, Ric Flair takes Curt Hennig as his partner and defeats Konnan and Syxx of the New World Order (nWo). Tony Schiavone and Dusty Rhodes speculate during commentary - - "Are we seeing the next member of the Four Horseman?" But again, Hennig declines.

Arn Anderson and Curt Hennig shake hands as Hennig becomes a Horseman.

However, weeks later, one of the most emotional nights in Four Horsemen history takes place on the 8/25 "Monday Nitro" from Columbia, SC. First, Ric Flair, Steve McMichael, and Chris Benoit demand an answer from Curt Hennig on whether he will accept a position in the Horsemen or not. Hennig, as he has done for well over a month now, tells Flair he's not ready to give that answer. Flair says he anticipated Hennig's position and asks Arn Anderson to come down to the ring. It is Arn's first appearance back in WCW since the spring when he left to have neck surgery, a procedure that has left him unable to wrestle again. It is a big moment both in the storyline and behind the scenes as this is Arn Anderson's real-life retirement from the ring. Ric Flair is very emotional as Arn tells the crowd his career as a wrestler is over.

But Arn says he has one more thing to do as his last official act as a Horsemen. He offers Curt Hennig, not just "a spot" in the Horsemen, he offers Hennig *his* spot. Hennig, obviously moved by the moment and taken by Arn's gesture, tells Arn it would be a privilege. He shakes Arn's hand, and raises the four-fingers and becomes a member of the Four Horseman.

But the fix was in.

SEPTEMBER 1997

One of the worst betrayals in the history of the Horsemen takes place at the "Fall Brawl" pay-per-view event on 9/14 in Winston-Salem, NC. It happens during a War Games match between members of the New World Order (Kevin Nash, Buff Bagwell, Syxx, and Konnan) and the Four Horsemen (Ric Flair, Steve McMichael, Chris Benoit, and new Horseman Curt Hennig.) Hennig enters the match last due to an apparent shoulder injury. However, only moments later it is revealed that the injury was simply subterfuge and Hennig has been allied with the nWo all along. Benoit and McMichael are handcuffed to the cage and Hennig and the nWo gang up on Flair. Benoit and McMichael refuse to give up for the team as the beating continues. Finally, as Nash threatens to slam the cage door onto Flair's head, Mongo submits, not wanting to see Flair suffer catastrophic injury. The match now over, Hennig betrays Flair a final time and slams his head in the cage door anyway. Kevin Nash proclaims it "the death of the Four Horsemen." It is one of the most devastating defeats for the Horsemen in their history.

Horsemen Title Change

The next night on Nitro, adding insult to injury, Curt Hennig defeats Steve McMichael for the U.S. title on 9/15 in Charlotte, NC. McMichael is described in this match as the "last Horseman standing," since Flair is out following the cage injury the previous night, Arn is retired following neck surgery, and Benoit is out of action following a concussion in War Games. Hennig injures Mongo's knee in the match where he wins the U.S. title, and the following week, for the first time in years, not a single member of the Horsemen is on Nitro.

Two weeks later (9/29), Ric Flair calls in to Nitro by phone from his home in Charlotte and tells Tony Schiavone that he is breaking up the Horsemen. He says he has too much respect for Benoit and Mongo to ask them to fight his fights for him, and pleads with them to go their own way. The Horsemen as a unit go dormant once again until the final reformation in 1998.

1998

APRIL 1998
Behind the scenes, Ric Flair is fired by Eric Bischoff after a disagreement between the two over whether Ric was granted time off to attend his son's amateur wrestling event. Flair missed a live "WCW Thunder" broadcast, and Bischoff decided to make an example out of him. The result was nearly five months of a behind-the-scenes legal battle between Flair and WCW, as well as fans chanting "We Want Flair" more weeks than not on Nitro and Thunder broadcasts.

The "Wrestling Observer" newsletter (4/20/98, 9/7/98) reported that the original plans for the episode of "WCW Thunder" that Flair missed were for Flair to announce yet another reformation of the Four Horsemen, which had been dormant since the Curt Hennig betrayal in September of 1997. Reportedly, the group was to include Flair, Bill Goldberg, former Horsemen Lex Luger, and NFL star Kevin Greene, managed by Arn Anderson. (It's not clear why Chris Benoit would have been excluded from this reformation. Steve McMichael was not active with WCW at this time.)

Instead, with Flair now fired, the final reformation of the Four Horsemen took another path.

MAY – JULY 1998
For the next several months, WCW would tease a Horsemen reunion without Flair even being in the company. Benoit and McMichael reunited and attempted to convince Arn Anderson to put the group back together.

Dean Malenko joined in this effort as well, beginning on the 7/17 episode of "WCW Thunder," asking Arn to be an advisor to him and his now steady tag team partner Chris Benoit. But Arn continually refused all of them.

But then Malenko made the mistake of holding up four fingers and suggesting Arn come out of retirement himself and put the Horsemen back together. It didn't sit well with Arn, who bore the scars of a surgery that took his in-ring career away from him:

> "Don't presume you can stick four fingers in my face and get my attention, because you ain't earned the right. None of you get it! You don't think I have the passion for this? ... I've got the heart, but I don't have the tools. So I'm telling you; if you've got any humanity left in your body, just let it be." – Arn Anderson

AUGUST 1998

What began to turn Arn around was an emotional moment that took place on the 8/31 edition of "Monday Nitro" when James J. Dillon confronted him with a special video that Dillon said he had pulled from his personal video collection. The video was of Arn Anderson in the early spring of 1985 standing on a beach in Pensacola, FL, announcing he was on his way to join Jim Crockett Promotions. Dillon asks Arn to reunite the Horsemen one last time, to fight for WCW in their battles with the various factions of the nWo. Steve McMichael and Chris Benoit join in the plea, but an emotional Anderson walks away once again.

SEPTEMBER 1998

A week later on the 9/7 Nitro, watching the nWo try to slam Dean Malenko's head in the door of a steel cage following a match with Curt Hennig, Arn has had enough and makes the dramatic save, his first time in a physical confrontation since returning to television and announcing his retirement in August of 1997.

The attack on Malenko that was so eerily similar to what he had witnessed happen to his best friend, Ric Flair, a year ago at "Fall Brawl," had forced Arn to change his mind. After months of refusing to consider it, he finally decides to reunite the Horsemen.

Behind the scenes, Ric Flair settles matters legally with WCW and he is finally able to return to the company.

It all leads to one of the most memorable and emotional reunions of the Horsemen since their inception.

REFORMATION #4
(Dean Malenko & the Return of Ric Flair)

Ric Flair returns to WCW television on "Monday Nitro" on 9/14 in Greenville, SC. James J. Dillon first brings out Arn Anderson, who then introduces each of the Four Horsemen one by one, all of them dressed in black for the special occasion. Dillon was the original leader of the Four Horsemen going back to their inception thirteen years earlier. He is now passing that torch to Arn Anderson, who becomes the new leader and manager of the group.

Arn introduces Steve McMichael, then Chris Benoit - - and then Dean Malenko. This would actually be Dean Malenko's first official night as a member of the Four Horsemen.

> "Dean Malenko, I've been yakking out here for the last ten years about what it meant to be a Horseman – work ethic, respect for the business, respect for each other, respect for the people that came before us - - and while I was yakking, you were out there fighting the fight for the Horsemen. I said that you didn't get it. Well, I didn't get it, because if there was ever a Horsemen, it makes me a little misty eyed and real proud to call you on this day the finest thing you can be in the sport of professional wrestling, and that's a Horseman."
>
> – Arn Anderson

As Arn begins to celebrate this reunion, he suddenly stops and says, "Wait a minute. What a goof! I almost forgot the fourth Horsemen - - - Ric Flair!"

And with that, the roof nearly comes off the building, as for the first time in five months, Ric Flair 'walks the aisle' again. He enters the ring in tears to a huge ovation and embraces each of the Horsemen, lingering an extra moment or two in a long hug with Arn Anderson.

Flair talks to the Greenville crowd about how much it means to him to be back, especially in that city, where so many of his roots are firmly planted in the old Mid-Atlantic territory.

Suddenly, he is interrupted by Eric Bischoff and the two have a heated exchange.

"Fire me! I'm already fired! Fire me! I'm already fired!"
– Ric Flair

But nothing can take the sparkle off of what proves to be one of the most memorable moments in WCW history. Tony Schiavone calls it "the greatest night in the history of our sport."

The final reformation of the Four Horsemen is complete. But there is one more wrinkle yet to take place in a couple of months with one of the most famous Horsemen from years ago.

OCTOBER 1998

In the weeks that follow the reunion, the Horsemen are on a roll, flexing their muscles and wielding their regained power. They back down Bischoff and the nWo on several different occasions over the next weeks. Chris Benoit and Dean Malenko continue as a regular tag team managed by Arn Anderson. Flair has his sights set on another world championship, but Eric Bischoff says he still has the ultimate power, and refuses to let Flair wrestle.

NOVEMBER 1998

A scenario involving one of the classic members of the Horsemen from the past plays out over the month of November on "Monday Nitro."

On 11/16 from Wichita, KS, Ric Flair talks with Gene Okerlund about tradition and says he has a surprise for Eric Bischoff.

> *"I want to introduce a man, who in my estimation, is one of the greatest wrestlers alive. A Horseman of yester-year, a Horseman of today. Barry Windham, come on down!"*
> *– Ric Flair*

He brings out Barry Windham, who is making a return to WCW. Windham holds up the four-fingers as he walks to the ring. Flair and Windham celebrate as speculation begins as to whether Windham will become a Horseman again.

The next week on 11/23, Bischoff tells Flair he doesn't have the power to hire whomever he wants, and Flair responds that Windham was a Horseman in the past, and that if he wants to be, he will be again. Bischoff laughs and tells Flair he doesn't understand - - it is Eric Bischoff that has all the power. And with that cue, Windham turns on Flair and the two brawl. Windham reveals himself to be the paid henchman of Bischoff and the nWo. Flair is outraged and demands a wrestling match with Bischoff himself.

The following week 11/30, Bischoff finally agrees to wrestle Flair, but only if Dean Malenko can defeat his guy Barry Windham in a match later that night. However, Bischoff assigns nWo member Dusty Rhodes as the special referee. Dusty promises to call the match right down the middle and then smiles at Windham, so Bischoff is confident that the fix is in. However, Rhodes disqualifies Windham when he repeatedly won't break in the corner while working over Malenko's leg. Bischoff is incensed and orders Windham to attack Rhodes as Dusty is leaving the ring area, but the Horsemen storm down the aisle and all four (Flair, Malenko, Benoit, and McMichael) intercept Windham and dole out justice for turning his back on the Four Horsemen. It's an old-fashion beat down just like the Horsemen were famous for in the 1980s.

Pro Wrestling Illustrated / Kappa Publishing

Rhodes' disqualification of Windham means Flair finally gets his match with Bischoff, which is set to take place at "Starrcade '98."

DECEMBER 1998
On "WCW Thunder" in December, Bischoff antagonizes Flair by beating up on Flair's sons David and Reid and even kisses Flair's wife Beth. As a result, Flair is becoming more crazed and deranged with each passing week.

On 12/27 the unthinkable happens as Eric Bischoff defeats Ric Flair at "Starrcade '98" in Washington DC. Flair simply demolishes Bischoff for most of the match and has him in the figure four, but referee Charles Robinson, who had been knocked down earlier, can't hear Bischoff submit. Suddenly Curt Hennig, who was making a surprise return after being out of action for several months with an injury, appears at ringside and hands Bischoff a foreign object. Bischoff knocks Flair out, revives the referee, and covers Flair for the three count.

The next night at "Monday Nitro" in Baltimore, MD, Flair is completely out of his mind demanding that Bischoff wrestle him one more time. Flair says he will sign over his house, cars, and give Bischoff all of his worldly possessions if he'll face him that night in the Baltimore Arena. He starts taking off his clothing and eventually winds up in nothing but his boxer shorts, handcuffed to the ring-ropes! It is one of the wilder scenes in the history of Nitro.

Flair offers the following stipulations: if Bischoff wins, Flair will leave WCW forever. But if Flair wins, he will get control of WCW for 90 days.

Bischoff agrees to the stipulations and the match is set as the main event that night in Baltimore. With Flair waiting on him in the ring, Bischoff gets cold feet and tries to leave the building, but when he gets in his limousine, he finds all of the other Horsemen there waiting for him and they carry him to the ring.

Flair dominates the short match, but as he is preparing to take Bischoff out, members of the nWo storm the ring. The Horsemen hold them at bay, allowing Flair to eventually apply the figure four and Bischoff submits. Flair celebrates in the ring with the WCW contingent, and even Tony Schiavone and Dusty Rhodes are in the ring to celebrate with him as well. Flair now will be President of WCW.

If Windham's turn a month earlier and the loss to Bischoff at Starrcade were low points for the Nature Boy, this final Nitro of 1998 is certainly one of the high moments. And as it would turn out, it is one of the last shining moments for the Horsemen as a cohesive unit as well, as 1999 would start a slow decline on the way to the Four Horsemen's final chapter.

1999

After a strong finish to 1998, the Four Horsemen begin to disintegrate in 1999. Steve "Mongo" McMichael suffers a legit foot injury in early February and is released from the company. Flair goes mad with power as President of WCW. He seemingly wants less and less to do with the Horsemen, and prefers teaming with and managing the affairs of his son David. Chris Benoit and Dean Malenko are becoming increasingly frustrated with Flair. Arn Anderson is caught in the middle of all of it as usual, trying to hold the group together.

Dean Malenko and Chris Benoit capture the WCW World Tag Team title for the Horsemen.

MARCH 1999

Horsemen Title Change

Despite the uneasiness within the group, it is a huge night for the Four Horsemen at the "Uncensored" pay-per-view event in Louisville, KY:

(1) Ric Flair (with Arn Anderson) defeats Hulk Hogan in a first blood, steel cage match to win the WCW World championship for the 14th time.

(2) In a battle of current Horsemen vs. former Horsemen, Chris Benoit and Dean Malenko (with Arn Anderson) defeat Barry Windham and

Curt Hennig in a lumberjack match to win the WCW World Tag Team championship. (Windham and Hennig had defeated Benoit and Malenko in the finals of a tournament on 2/21 in Oakland, CA, to win the vacant titles.)

Horsemen Title Change
Two weeks later on the 3/29 "Monday Nitro" in Toronto, ON, Rey Mysterio, Jr. and Billy Kidman defeat Benoit and Malenko for the tag team belts.

APRIL 1999
Horsemen Title Change
Ric Flair loses the WCW title in a 4-way match to Diamond Dallas Page that also includes Hulk Hogan and Sting. The match takes place on 4/11 at the "Spring Stampede" pay-per-view event in Tacoma, WA. It is the last championship to be held by a member of the Four Horsemen while the Horsemen were still in existence.

MAY 1999
The new World Tag Team champions are Perry Saturn and Raven by virtue of a win at "Slamboree" on 5/9 in a three-way match with Dean Malenko, Chris Benoit and the former champs Rey Mysterio and Billy Kidman. The Horsemen are intent on regaining their world tag team championship, but the man still currently in charge of WCW, Ric Flair, doesn't seem interested in helping them get a title rematch.

> *"Chris, you know what it is? You've got to take care of yourself and I've got to take care of myself. The only way we're going to move in this company is do it our own way."*
> – *Dean Malenko*

On the 5/24 episode of "Monday Nitro" from Greenville, SC, Flair awards a title shot at the upcoming "Great American Bash" pay-per-view to Diamond Dallas Page & Bam Bam Bigelow after the members of Page's "Jersey Triad" help Flair out of a jam earlier with Roddy Piper. Malenko and Benoit are unhappy about it, feeling as though Flair should have given the title shot to them. Arn Anderson tries to smooth things out as usual, but with Flair totally absorbed in pushing his son David, this time things seem different. Malenko and Benoit, already frustrated with their position in the company, have now finally had it with Flair.

Later in that same Nitro, Roddy Piper challenges Ric Flair, Dallas Page, and Bam Bam Bigelow (part of the Jersey Triad) to a six-man tag match, where Piper will have two mystery partners. Malenko and Benoit walk down the ramp and Flair thinks the boys are coming to help him out, but in a shocking development, Benoit and Malenko are revealed as Roddy Piper's mystery partners. They indeed have had enough.

If there is one defining moment in time to mark as the end of the Four Horsemen, it is this. Benoit and Malenko leave the group. It only leaves Flair, with Arn at his side. The Horsemen are dead.

Chis Benoit and Dean Malenko subsequently head out on their own in WCW, eventually forging a new alliance in late July with Perry Saturn and Shane Douglas known as "The Revolution," a group that traced its origins back to the original ECW promotion.

Arn Anderson remains loyal to Ric Flair in later skirmishes with Malenko, Benoit, and others. Anderson and Flair make occasional Horsemen references in their interviews and promos. After all, they have been members of the group since it all originally came together back in 1985, and will consider themselves Horsemen forever. But the final era of the Four Horsemen as an entity has ended, and the group would never resurrect itself again. ◆

WCW MONDAY NITRO TNT

CHAPTER SEVEN
Reflections

There were a total of twelve distinct versions of the Four Horsemen over a thirteen year period. This included two versions where there were only three members of the group (most notably with Paul Roma in 1993) and a version where there were five (with Jeff Jarrett in 1997.)

Along the way there were several times where the Horsemen were in transition and had fewer than four members, including a time when there were briefly just two (Ric Flair and Barry Windham with J.J. in 1988-1989.) These transitional periods are not included in the official versions of the Horsemen. However, they are reflected in the 5-page summary chart in chapter two that tracks additions and subtractions to the group for everyone involved, including the women who were linked with the group at various times.

It might be fair to classify the version with Kendall Windham in 1989 as a transitional period rather than an official version of the Horsemen, but to do so would eliminate Kendall from inclusion in any official version on this list, and since he was briefly an official member of the group, he deserves to be included in this list. His tenure, however, surely represents the shortest-lived version of the Horsemen at only one week in length.

DIRTY DOZEN: THE VERSIONS OF THE HORSEMEN

ERA	VERSION	YEARS	MEMBERS
Crockett	1	1985-1986	Ric Flair, Arn Anderson, Ole Anderson, Tully Blanchard (managed by James J. Dillon)
Crockett	2	1987	Ric Flair, Arn Anderson, Tully Blanchard, Lex Luger (managed by James J. Dillon)
Crockett	3	1988	Ric Flair, Arn Anderson, Tully Blanchard, Barry Windham (managed by James J. Dillon)
Crockett	4	1989	Ric Flair, Barry Windham, Kendall Windham (managed by James J. Dillon)
Early WCW	5	1989-1990	Ric Flair, Arn Anderson, Ole Anderson, Sting
Early WCW	6	1990-1991	Ric Flair, Arn Anderson, Barry Windham, Sid Vicious (managed by Ole Anderson)
Early WCW	7	1993	Ric Flair, Arn Anderson, Paul Roma
Monday Nitro	8	1995-1996	Ric Flair, Arn Anderson, Brian Pillman, Chris Benoit
Monday Nitro	9	1996-1997	Ric Flair, Arn Anderson, Chris Benoit, Steve McMichael
Monday Nitro	10	1997	Ric Flair, Arn Anderson, Chris Benoit, Steve McMichael, Jeff Jarrett
Monday Nitro	11	1997	Ric Flair, Chris Benoit, Steve McMichael, Curt Hennig (managed by Arn Anderson)
Monday Nitro	12	1998-1999	Ric Flair, Chris Benoit, Steve McMichael, Dean Malenko (managed by Arn Anderson)

There were also periods of time where an active member of the Horsemen was out of action for an extended period of time due to injury, but remained a part of the group. Examples include Ole Anderson's worked injury in 1986, and both Ric Flair and Arn Anderson's legitimate injuries in 1997.

The only person to be a wrestling member of each of the twelve versions of the Horsemen was Ric Flair, and so it is fair to say (and was indeed said several times over the final years of the group) that without Ric Flair in the mix, the Four Horsemen would not exist.

THE ENFORCER

Arn Anderson was a member of all twelve versions, but was not a wrestler in all twelve, and served in a managerial role for the final two. But to me, it is equally fair to say that without Arn Anderson, there could be no Four Horsemen. Throughout all of their existence, Arn was the heart and soul of the group. He was the guy that worked the hardest to keep the group together during the times there was dissension in the ranks. This includes enforcing a certain standard of membership when both Ole Anderson and Lex Luger were kicked out in the 1980s, and working as an 'elder statesman' in attempt to hold the group together in the mid-to-late 1990s.

Arn was also largely responsible for the original formation of the Horsemen, effectively naming them in 1985, as well as the key to each of the four reformations of the Horsemen over the years. In 1989, the first reformation took place when Arn made his dramatic return to WCW at Center Stage in Atlanta. Then in 1993, he embraced Paul Roma as a tag team partner and won a World championship with him when fans never looked at Roma as worthy of being a Horseman.

When Ric and Arn had their brief split during a period of dormancy in 1995, it was Arn who spearheaded the third

MANAGING THE HORSEMEN
Leadership within Wrestling's Greatest Stable

James J. Dillon	1985-1989, 1998*	Originally the Executive Director of Tully Blanchard Enterprises, became the leader of the Four Horsemen. Passed the torch to Arn Anderson in 1998.
Ole Anderson	1990, 1993*	Took the leadership roll after both Barry Windham returned and Sid Vicious joined in 1990. Helped re-form the Horsemen in 1993.
Arn Anderson	1997, 1998-1999	Briefly in the leadership role after giving his spot to Curt Hennig in 1997. Became the leader of the Horsemen after putting them back together upon Ric Flair's return in 1998. Torch passed to him from James J. Dillon.

*ONE NIGHT ONLY

reformation with friend Brian Pillman, and they were later joined by Flair when he pulled the big swerve on Sting at Halloween Havoc.

And of course the most famous and meaningful reformation of all was finally put together by Arn that famous night in Greenville, SC, when Flair returned to the company. Several former members of the group including Chris Benoit, Steve McMichael, and even James J. Dillon urged Arn for months to get the Horsemen back together. It couldn't happen unless Arn was the one to do it. And of course, Arn knew he couldn't do it without the group being once again anchored around Flair.

Arn was also the most loyal, at least to Flair. When Ric was losing his mind in the storylines in the last year or so of the Horsemen, Arn remained loyal, even at the expense of the Horsemen falling apart at the very end.

THE WOMEN

At different points in time throughout the years, various women played important roles in support of the Four Horsemen. Most commonly referred to as valets, they were much more than that defined role. There are countless key moments throughout the in-ring history of the Four Horsemen where their actions had a decisive impact on match finishes and title changes. Baby Doll turning on Dusty Rhodes in 1986 to allow Ric Flair to retain his World championship is one example. Miss Elizabeth turning on Randy Savage is another, where she loaned Flair one of her high-heeled shoes as a foreign object to aid him in regaining the World title.

And make no mistake, all five of the women officially associated with the Horsemen were gorgeous and proved to be distractions to the Horsemen's opponents. Sadly, some were also proven to be distractions within the Horsemen themselves. Benoit's romantic relationship with Woman proved to exacerbate the Horsemen's adversarial relationship with Kevin Sullivan. And there was always drama surrounding the actions of Debra McMichael, who encouraged bringing trouble-maker Jeff Jarrett into the Horsemen. She eventually left her husband for Jarrett in what was one of the worst periods of dissension within the ranks of the group.

But regardless of how it played out, the women of the Four Horsemen were always an intriguing part of the story.

LENDING A HELPING HAND

There are some very memorable moments in Horsemen history that involved people who were not officially associated with the group, but who played a key role in certain matches or storylines through the years.

Many of them were wrestlers who stepped in at critical times to aid the Horsemen in certain key matches involving the group

WOMEN OF THE HORSEMEN
The Valets, Queens, and Perfect 10's That Rode Along

Baby Doll	1985, 1986	Tully Blanchard's "Perfect 10" when the Horsemen were formed. She turned on Dusty Rhodes to rejoin the group for a short time.
Dark Journey	1987	Hired by James J. Dillon to be Tully Blanchard's "personal secretary" for Tully Blanchard Enterprises.
Woman	1990, 1996-1997	Started hanging with the Horsemen after stalking Ric Flair in 1990. Joined the group again in 1996 and became the romantic interest of Chris Benoit.
Miss Elizabeth	1996	Turned on Randy Savage to accompany the Four Horsemen until forced to join the nWo.
Queen Debra	1996-1997	Married to Horseman Steve "Mongo" McMichael, she turned on her husband to hook up with Jeff Jarrett.

as a whole. The most notable of these were wrestlers who took the place of an injured Horseman in War Games events. It first happened in 1987 when James J. Dillon enlisted the aid of a huge masked wrestler known as "War Machine" to take his place in the War Games event in the Orange Bowl during the Great American Bash tour that year. In actuality, it was really Big Bubba Rogers on loan from the stable of the Midnight Express from manager Jim Cornette. In 1991, Larry Zbyszko filled in for a legitimately injured Arn Anderson as the Horsemen battled Sting, the Steiner brothers, and future Horseman Brian Pillman.

And then there were those that lent a helping hand by simply teaming with the Horsemen in their battles with other factions. Examples of this included teaming with the Dungeon of Doom to battle Hulk Hogan in 1996, and teaming with Roddy Piper to battle the nWo in 1997.

LENDING A HAND
Those Who Helped Out the Horsemen on Occasion

War Machine (Big Bubba Rogers)	July 1987	Teamed with the Horsemen in War Games at the Orange Bowl in Miami replacing an injured J.J. Dillon.
"Shogun" Hiro Matsuda	Oct. 1987	Hired by J.J. Dillon to help Lex Luger prepare for his U.S. title defense against Dusty Rhodes. Later bought the contracts of the Horsemen.
Ronnie Garvin & Gary Hart	July 1988	Garvin was paid by James J. Dillon and Gary Hart to turn heel and interfere in Windham's U.S. title defense against Dusty Rhodes. Hart became his manager.
Minnesota Wrecking Crew II (Mike Enos & Wayne Bloom)	March 1990	Ole Anderson's masked tag-team that takes up the battle vs. the Steiner Brothers while Arn Anderson is out with an injury.
Harley Race	July 1990	Teamed with Barry Windham in Horsemen tag team matches on house shows, filling in for an injured Ric Flair.
Larry Zbyszko	Feb. 1991	Teamed with the Horsemen in War Games at Wrestle War '91 filling in for an injured Arn Anderson.
Jimmy Hart	Dec. 1995	Accompanied Ric Flair for several weeks, including Flair's win over Randy Savage for the WCW World title at Starrcade '95.
Dungeon of Doom	March 1996	Teamed with the Horsemen in a Doomsday Cage match to form the "Alliance to End Hulkamania."
Bobby Heenan	June 1996	Acted as special coach for Ric Flair and Arn Anderson in their tag match with NFL stars Kevin Greene and Steve McMichael at Bash '96.
Roddy Piper	March 1997	Teamed with the Horsemen in a triangle match vs. Team WCW and Team nWo at Uncensored.
Charles Robinson	1999	Ric Flair's personal referee for matches while he was President of WCW.

Others provided a service such as the time the "Shogun" Hiro Matsuda helped Lex Luger prepare for his U.S. title defense against Dusty Rhodes in 1987, or when Charles Robinson became Ric Flair's personal referee in 1999.

And sometimes even wrestling's true elite pitched in, as was the case in 1990 when former 8-time NWA World Heavyweight champion Harley Race filled in for a legitimately injured Ric Flair, teaming with Barry Windham against Sting and Lex Luger in tag team matches in several cities.

Some famous wrestling managers also lent a hand. Gary Hart formed a secret alliance with James J. Dillon in 1988 that convinced Ron Garvin to turn on Dusty Rhodes and help Barry Windham retain the United States title against Rhodes at the Great American Bash.

Jimmy Hart accompanied Ric Flair in late 1995 and early 1996, as both had common enemies in the Dungeon of Doom. He was with the Horsemen at Starrcade when Flair defeated Randy Savage for the World title after winning a triangle match with Luger and Sting. Hart's interests, however, were with The Giant and that was borne out later in 1996 when he managed the Giant in his shocking upset over Ric Flair to win the WCW World title.

Bobby Heenan also helped out the Horsemen at the Great American Bash in 1996 when he was the "coach" for the team of Flair and Anderson against the NFL all-star team of Kevin Greene and Steve McMichael. It was in that match that McMichael joined the Horsemen.

CHAMPIONSHIP GOLD

Of course, part of being a Horseman, especially in the early years, was having championship gold around your waist. In later years, championships weren't as big a part of the Horsemen story as the boys seemed more focused on the infighting within the

HORSEMEN CHAMPIONSHIPS
Titles Held While a Member of the Four Horsemen

WORLD HEAVYWEIGHT CHAMPIONSHIP
Ric Flair (Multiple occasions over his 13 years in the Horsemen.)

WORLD TAG TEAM CHAMPIONSHIP
Tully Blanchard & Arn Anderson (1987, 1988)
Arn Anderson & Paul Roma (1993)
Dean Malenko & Chris Benoit (1999)

UNITED STATES HEAVYWEIGHT CHAMPIONSHIP
Tully Blanchard (1985)
Lex Luger (1987)
Barry Windham (1988)
Ric Flair (1996)
Jeff Jarrett (1997)
Steve McMichael (1997)

NATIONAL HEAVYWEIGHT CHAMPIONSHIP
Tully Blanchard (1986)

NATIONAL TAG TEAM CHAMPIONSHIP
Ole & Arn Anderson (1985)

TV CHAMPIONSHIP
Arn Anderson (1986, 1990, 1991)
Tully Blanchard (1986)

group and trying to battle other factions like the nWo. But in the Crockett Era of the Horsemen, it was all about the championship gold.

Perhaps the best example of this was the third version of the Four Horsemen in 1988. During their five months together, they held all of the top titles in the NWA. Ric Flair, of course, maintained his dominance of the World Heavyweight title as he had for the past seven years. Tully Blanchard and Arn Anderson held the NWA World Tag Team titles that they originally won in

Pro Wrestling Illustrated / Kappa Publishing

the fall of 1987 from the Rock and Roll Express and had recently regained from Barry Windham and Lex Luger the night Barry Windham became a Horseman. And weeks after joining the group, Barry Windham won the United States championship in the tournament held in Houston, TX, to fill the vacant title, left open when Dusty Rhodes had been stripped of the belt. This version of the Four Horsemen is largely considered by fans to be the greatest version of the Horsemen ever assembled, and certainly represents them at their championship peak.

The title most frequently held by the Horsemen was the famed United States championship. Six different members of the Horsemen held the title from the years 1985 through 1997, including Ric Flair who held the title a record 6 times over a nineteen year period from 1977 through 1996.

Fittingly, the last title held by a member of the Four Horsemen was the WCW World title held by Ric Flair, who lost the title to Diamond Dallas Page in April of 1999 in a four-way match that also included Sting and Hulk Hogan. ◆

"Diamonds are forever, and so are the Four Horsemen."
- Ric Flair

CHAPTER EIGHT
Legacy

It's often been said (including in the opening pages of this book) that the Four Horsemen set the stage for every other 'faction' or 'stable' of wrestlers that followed. That's certainly true in the modern era of wrestling, and the use of a faction as an element in booking certainly came about after the success of the Horsemen. Groups and gangs had existed before, of course, usually centered on their manager (for example, Bobby Heenan's stable in the AWA in the 1970s.) But on a national stage, the Four Horsemen were the first and without a doubt the most talked about group in wrestling history.

There have been many great factions that have followed them. Two of them that seemed to be so much in the mold of the Horsemen were the Dangerous Alliance in WCW and Evolution in the WWE.

Just as all versions of the Four Horsemen are linked together by Ric Flair and Arn Anderson, these two factions also have that Flair/Anderson connection. Arn was a member of Paul E.

Dangerously's Dangerous Alliance, along with Bobby Eaton, Ricky Steamboat, Rick Rude, and Larry Zbyzsko. Years later, Triple H (a huge fan of the Four Horsemen growing up) put together a stable called Evolution that consisted of himself, Randy Orton, Dave Batista, and Ric Flair. In that group, Flair played the role of the experienced elder statesman that Ole Anderson had played in the original version of the Horsemen.

There are, of course, other famous factions like the nWo and DX, but as Jim Ross has said on so many occasions, none of these would have likely existed in the manner in which they did without the Four Horsemen paving the way before them.

In 2012, the group was inducted into the WWE Hall of Fame. The version of the Horsemen that was inducted is considered, by fans at least, the greatest line-up of Horsemen of them all: Ric Flair, Arn Anderson, Tully Blanchard, Barry Windham, and their leader James J. Dillon. It was a special night to see them back together after so many years, and in Flair's case, it was his second time being inducted into the WWE Hall of Fame. He went in as an individual wrestler in the Class of 2008.

The choice of that particular version ignited a discussion among fans as to just which version of the Horsemen was the best, and which version was most deserving of the Hall of Fame recognition. It was reported that the WWE tired to include Ole Anderson, but Ole declined to appear.

Any discussion of this, by the way, is usually limited to the three main versions of the Horsemen during the Crockett Era, when they were unquestionably the top heels and the main focus of the booking in Jim Crockett Promotions.

Those three versions can be called the Ole version, the Luger version, and the Windham version. All three versions have their ardent supporters. For some it is a matter of their favorite version as opposed to the best. As for your own personal favorite, well that's up to you. As for the *best* version, it usually comes down to only two from the originals.

OTHER MEMBERSHIPS
Horsemen That Went On To Other Factions in WCW & WWE*

Name	Years	Faction
Ric Flair	2001	Magnificent Seven
	2003-2005	Evolution
Arn Anderson	1988-1989	Heenan Family
	1991-1992	Dangerous Alliance
Tully Blanchard	1988-1989	Heenan Family
Lex Luger	1998-1999	New World Order (nWo)
	2000	Millionaire's Club
	2001	Magnificent Seven
Barry Windham	1997	Jim Cornette's NWA Stable
	1998	New World Order (nWo)
	1999	West Texas Rednecks
Kendall Windham	1999	West Texas Rednecks
Sting	1998	New World Order (nWo)
	2000	Millionaire's Club
Sid Vicious	2000	Millionaire's Club
Brian Pillman	1997	Hart Foundation
Chris Benoit	1999-2000	Revolution
	2001	Radicalz
Jeff Jarrett	1997	Jim Cornette's NWA Stable
	1999	New World Order (nWo)
	2000	New Blood
	2001	Magnificent Seven
Curt Hennig	1997-1999	New World Order (nWo)
	1999	West Texas Rednecks
	2000	Millionaire's Club
Dean Malenko	1999-2000	Revolution
	2001	Radicalz

*WCW and WWE factions only. Dates are approximate.

It's hard to argue against the Windham version strictly from the standpoint of championships the group held. But I would argue that the original Ole Anderson version was the best, hands down. And I'm not alone in that assessment, as all four of the original members, as well as manager James J. Dillon, have stated the same at one time or another. You would expect Ole to have that opinion, but Ric and Arn have stated so as well. Of course, they are prone to change their mind depending on when they are asked or the context of the discussion.

Let's be fair: it's hard for any group, be it in wrestling, music, or mainstream sports, to follow the original, especially when the originals are so iconic and successful.

For longtime wrestling fans - - and for purposes of this discussion I'm talking about people who were fans in the 1970s and earlier - - Ole Anderson was the validating force in the Four Horsemen. He was the rock. If you grew up watching wrestling in the Mid-Atlantic and Georgia territories, there was hardly anyone more believable, both on the microphone and in the ring, than Ole Anderson. Fans who weren't afforded the opportunity to see Ole's work week in and week out in those years may not get that.

Ole was a big mouth, a bully, a braggart, but he backed it up in the ring. You hated him, but couldn't help but eventually admire him. He and Gene Anderson would do anything to keep their tag team championship belts, and after watching them do it year after year, you eventually garnered a matter of respect for them.

Of course, all of the original Horsemen were great at talking you into the building. Their interview and promo segments on the various wrestling programs were often just as much or more fun than the wrestling itself.

In the end, it's really not that important as to which version was better than the others. What is generally accepted is that the Horsemen of the 1980s, of the Crockett Era, was the best stable of wrestlers ever.

If you enjoy reliving some of these memories, it's fun to watch the 2007 documentary portion of the WWE DVD collection "Ric Flair and the Four Horsemen." It lays out pretty well the entire history of the Horsemen and lets you enjoy some of the many magical moments, particularly in those early years. A majority of the members of the Horsemen are included in commentary as well.

It's also worth checking out their 2012 WWE Hall of Fame induction. It is in the "Originals" on-demand section on the WWE Network.

The WWE Network also has within its archives many of the programs that featured the Four Horsemen's story over their thirteen years, in particular Jim Crockett's "World Championship Wrestling" that aired on Superstation WTBS in the 1980s and "WCW Monday Nitro" that aired on the TNT Network in the 1990s. However, there is a large amount of TV not included there, especially the better early material that is found on the syndicated programs of Jim Crockett promotions such as "NWA Pro Wrestling" and "World Wide Wrestling." Hopefully they will eventually see the light of day on the network.

While the early stuff is particularly fun to watch again and stands the test of time, there isn't a whole lot after the Crockett Era I enjoy seeing again. There are a few exceptions. I enjoyed the rare moments where the Horsemen showed real unity in the later years, such as the time Arn Anderson joined Chris Benoit in putting the boots to Kevin Sullivan in a cathartic moment at the Great American Bash in 1996. It was also fun to get the occasional surprise such as when Steve "Mongo" McMichael turned on Kevin Green, slammed that Halliburton briefcase into his head, and became the fourth Horsemen, also at that same Bash event. Being a fan of the Chicago Bears, that was particularly fun for me to see.

There were times, too, when the Horsemen would refocus and get deadly serious like they had been in the past, such as when Barry Windham and Arn Anderson roamed the apocalyptic landscapes of junk yards and dangerous neighborhoods in early 1991 while preparing to challenge Doom for the tag team titles. There were the brilliant deceptions that almost worked like Barry Windham impersonating Sting to great effect in an attempt to rob him of his championship at Halloween Havoc '90.

Then of course there was Arn Anderson reuniting the Horsemen in 1998 in Greenville, SC, with the emotional return of Ric Flair. It is one of the great moments in wrestling history, period, much less just the history of the Four Horsemen.

The cover of the "Ric Flair and the Four Horsemen" DVD released by World Wrestling Entertainment in 2007.

Sometimes I wish that after the Horsemen went their separate ways in early 1989, that they never would have been resurrected, because they never were really given the chance to shine again like the original versions had. To their credit, the WWE never tried to re-form the Four Horsemen, although I suppose they still could in some fashion with second generation wrestlers like Charlotte Flair and Tessa Blanchard.

Charlotte Flair and her cohorts in NXT often referred to themselves as the Four Horsewomen. Those very close friends included Sasha Banks, Bayley, and Becky Lynch. A group of female fighters in the UFC led by Ronda Rousey also referred to themselves as the Four Horsewomen, often seen brandishing the four-finger salute. In the case of the latter, it is fascinating to see the legend of the Four Horsemen transcend sports and pop culture across two different generations.

While that four-finger salute was a constant part of being a Horsemen over their thirteen years, one of the great Horsemen traditions faded away after the early versions broke up. It was that demonstration of unity and brotherhood, most observable when they would all put their hands in together, all for one and one for all. That seemed to disappear early in the WCW era and was completely a distant memory during the Monday Nitro era, when disharmony seemingly was the norm every week. It was that loss of camaraderie that made those later versions of the Four Horsemen seem far less special.

Those early moments of solidarity and brotherhood are treasured all these years later. Ole Anderson's jubilant return in June of 1986 is, too this day, one of the greatest Horsemen moments ever.

There are so many special Horsemen moments to treasure: Ric Flair's bloody, but victorious, celebration as he stepped out of the cage at Starrcade '87, and Barry Windham holding the four-fingers and the mask of the Midnight Rider out of the window of the limousine. There were those great Horsemen beat-downs such as on Dusty in the cage in Atlanta, or punking the Road Warriors in the studios of WTBS, or ambushing Lex Luger as he got out of his limo at the Clash of Champions II. And there were more assaults on Ricky and Robert of the Rock and Roll Express than you can count.

As fans, we treasure those magic moments, the ones we like to play over and over on our old VCRs and DVD players, and relive countless times in our memories. It's where we can suspend our disbelief, get lost in the moment, and believe again. That's what makes wrestling special, and is what makes the Four Horsemen the most special of all. ◆

Wrestling

INTERVIEW 87: JESSE VENTURA "The Body" Speaks His Mind!

FROM THE PUBLISHERS OF PRO WRESTLING ILLUSTRATED

WRESTLING'S MOST DANGEROUS UNIT: THE FOUR HORSEMEN SUCCESS AT ANY PRICE!

PRO Wrestling ILLUSTRATED

WHY BIGELOW LEFT THE WWF
FULL-COLOR PINUP OF HACKSAW DUGGAN

THE FOUR HORSEMEN'S REVOLVING: WHO'S THE NEXT TO...

WCW Magazine

The Official Magazine of World Championship Wrestling
Issue 12 February 1996

RELIVE THE 4 HORSEMEN GLORY YEARS

"MACHO" CROWNED CHAMP !!!
WITNESS THE YEAR'S MOST INCREDIBLE EVENT

HOGAN vs S— is there more to c—

Catch the HOTTEST wrestling action on TV every week!
TBS SUPERSTATION

WCW Magazine

The Official Magazine of World Championship Wrestling
Issue 22

CAN THE HORSEMEN SURVIVE
FALL BRAWL
MAYHEM INSIDE

Catch the HOTTEST wrestling action on TV every week!
TBS SUPERSTATION

Made in the USA
Lexington, KY
06 January 2018